Prisoners On Purpose

A peacemakers' guide
to jails and prisons

A Nukewatch book

Edited by Samuel H. Day, Jr.
Illustrated by Bonnie Urfer

The Progressive Foundation
P.O. Box 2658
Madison, WI 53701

In association with
8th Day Center for Justice
1020 S. Wabash, Suite 680
Chicago, IL 60605

Prisoners on Purpose
A Peacemakers' guide to jails and prisons.

Library of Congress Catalog Card Number:89-062768

ISBN:0-942046-02-1

Book design by Bonnie Urfer and Maurice Thaler

Laser typography by Maurice Thaler, I/O Consulting

Manufactured in the United States of America

Contributors

Duane Bean	04973-045
Gail Beyer	
Bob Bossie	
Mike Bremer	05291-045
Samuel H. Day, Jr.	05121-045
Delany Dean	
Bill Douglas	
Janice Dover	
Dorothy Eber	04996-045
Jerry Ebner	04467-045
Katey Feit	05123-045
Ariel Glenn	04997-045
Sam Guardino	05122-045
Jean Gump	03789-045
Joe Gump	04468-045
Carl Kabat	03230-045
Barb Katt	
Kathy Kelly	04971-045
Mary Knebel	
John LaForge	
Betty Lewis	
Dan McGuire	
Larry Morlan	03788-045
Mike Stanek	05124-045
Bonnie Urfer	04970-045
Katie Willems	
Helen Woodson	03231-045
Jerry Zawada	04995-045

*Note: Some of the authors' names are followed by their eight-digit federal prison numbers. Each of these individuals contributed to this book while serving a sentence in a federal prison.

Contents

Foreword

IN 1986, WHILE I was still a prosecuting attorney, Jean Gump went to prison for a Missouri missile silo disarmament action. I had grown up on Air Force bases, the daughter of a pilot in the Strategic Air Command; without ever thinking about it, I believed in nuclear deterrence. It was an article of faith for so many of us during the Cold War years that the Soviet Union intended to bury us, and that the bloodthirsty Communists would be on our necks in a moment if we didn't maintain an arsenal of nuclear weapons, ready to destroy our enemies at any time. Until 1986, I saw no reason to question these beliefs.

Something changed in me after I read a Sunday newspaper feature about Jean Gump. It wasn't an instantaneous conversion; it was the beginning of a gradual awakening. I began to wonder what it was that had made Jean and those who acted with her so adamantly opposed to what seemed to me to be such a benevolent, necessary policy. Jean seemed to be a thoughtful, responsible human being; why was she in prison? As I read and reflected on the issues, the realization grew in me that our policy of "deterrence" is really a thinly disguised act of aggression directed not only toward the other nations of the earth, but also against the earth itself and all life. I began to understand why Jean went to prison.

In the summer of 1988 I met the Missouri Peace Planters. They occupied several Missouri missile silos in August and September, and it was my privilege to represent some of them at their trials in U.S. District Court. The pleasure and challenge of knowing these fine people have been accompanied by my sorrow in watching each of them sentenced, shackled, and led off to prison. And always we heard the familiar question, raised by family members, friends, judges, attorneys, sympathetic onlookers, Air Force personnel: "Why go to jail? Isn't there so much more you could accomplish on the outside?"

It seems like such folly, such waste! These are good people, people with strong values and deep commitment.

Some are kids you would love to have as your daughters or sons, some are older, the parents and grandparents of very fortunate and bewildered young people. They are in jails and prisons all over the United States, and they are doing some serious time; six months or a year or two years of their lives have been claimed by the United States government. What the Missouri Peace Planters have done is to challenge the federal government's lawless position that it can use the money, land, and other resources of the people of this nation for the purpose of threatening genocide against the peoples of this world. They went to the missile silos of Missouri to confront the gods of war and greed and national security. They went gently and unarmed, knowing that the soldiers and police, prosecutors and judges and jailers would come afterwards.

These Peace Planters didn't go to jail before they had explored other options. For years each of them had worked tirelessly in the outside world, using every available method to make their voices heard and to educate others about the threat of nuclear annihilation which hangs over all our heads. They supported and used the political process and mass media and leafleting and just plain talking to other people; they prayed. Over and over again, these dedicated people have confronted the massive denial in which we in this society live and move and breathe: we agree that it's awful and we must "do something," then we resume our discussion of where we will go out for dinner... We continue to pay our taxes.

Even before they went to jail, they swam upstream every stroke of the way, learning every day what Jesus meant when he told his friends that the world would hate them. They learned about weakness from their own experiences with the power structure, and from the experiences of Jesus and Gandhi and Martin Luther King, Jr. They knew very well that the early Christians were often called before the authorities and thrown in jail, even killed, for proclaiming some very unpopular truths. Their familiarity with the concepts of folly and uselessness grew. But they also remembered that Jesus reclaimed the Temple, and that King reclaimed the lunch counters and the buses and the voting booths for his people. They knew that they, too, were called to speak the truth in a very powerful way. The Missouri Peace Planters knew that they were called to reclaim the land.

It was only on rare occasions during the Peace Planter trials that the judges would permit those on trial to explain why they had gone to the silos. The prosecutors and judges had made it very clear that they were only interested in whether or not the defendants had gone onto government property without permission. But, from time to time, glimpses of truth would emerge. At some point or another each of the defendants managed to tell the court some part of his or her reason for being there. Patterns emerged: One terrible image which was often evoked was the memory of Nazi Germany, the quiet complicity of so many

German citizens in the brutal, systematic genocide perpetrated by their government. Many times the Peace Planters quietly and courteously told the court that they refused to be associated with or complicit in an even more devastating policy of genocide.

Why did they go to jail? Because they chose to set themselves completely and radically at odds with a government which has undertaken a totally unacceptable course of conduct. In refusing to accept the government's claim to the right to possess and make plans to use nuclear weapons, the Peace Planters became criminals in the eyes of that government. For each of them, it had finally become a simple proposition: When the government has become an outlaw, responsible citizens will go to prison. Sometimes, mere protest is inadequate; there comes a point at which, due to the immediacy and enormity of the danger, only a radical refusal to cooperate is appropriate. When we know that that time has come, we must totally withdraw our consent. And so, as a sign of contradiction to the rest of us who pay our taxes, enjoy the benefits of our wealthy society, and worry about the direction this nation is going in, the Peace Planters, those good and responsible people, have been imprisoned. Knowing this, we who are not yet imprisoned can see how much work there is left for us to do. In profound gratitude to our friends in prison, we will not forget.

Delany Dean
Kansas City, Missouri
August, 1989

Introduction

ON A MID-JULY weekend in 1988 about fifty people from a wide area of the Midwest gathered at a Catholic retreat center in Milwaukee, Wisconsin, to talk and pray about nuclear missiles.

They came from Chicago and its suburbs, from Milwaukee and Madison, and from Kansas City, the focal point of a growing concern about the 150 missile silos installed a quarter century earlier under the farms and fields of west central Missouri.

The retreat was a culmination of six months of earnest discussion among peace activists interested in raising the visibility of the long-buried "gods of metal" and heightening resistance to the national policy of nuclear deterrence embodied by the missiles, each a hundred times more destructive than the bomb that leveled Hiroshima.

For three days the participants worked and re-worked the ingredients of a plan to cut or climb their way past the high, barbed wire fences that surround the missile launch sites, which are unattended except by launch officers watching surveillance monitors in underground bunkers several miles away.

They struggled with philosophical and tactical issues: Should blood-pouring be allowed at the missile silos?

Should witnesses be permitted to accompany the activists who would be submitting themselves to arrest?

Seeking to school themselves in the way of nonviolence, they enacted skits dramatizing confrontations with nervous Air Force security patrols, with belligerent sheriff's officers, with cynical, hard-bitten jail inmates.

A priest led them in a "guided fantasy" from the missile site to the sheriff's office to the courtroom and to jail.

They hammered out a statement of principles and a manifesto which likened the weapons of nuclear annihilation to razor blades buried in the rich loaves of the North American breadbasket.

Amid song and prayer, and in hope and trepidation, the long retreat gave birth to Missouri Peace Planting '88—a plan to touch the nation's conscience by putting protesters in the path of nuclear missiles.

This would not be the first time peace activists had put their bodies on the lids of the launch tubes. More than a dozen had committed similar offenses in preceding years—and some had incurred lengthy prison terms for damaging silo covers and instruments. But the Missouri Peace Planting marked a significant escalation in numbers of people involved, in the breadth of participation, and in the openness of its summons to nonviolent resistance.

At dawn on Monday, August 15, following a weekend of preparations in which hundreds joined, a caravan of cars drove south from Kansas City, dropping off teams of activists and observers at missile launch sites in Bates, Cass, and St. Clair counties.

At precisely 7 a.m. the Peace Planters went to work. Some scaled the fences and others cut the padlocks on the gates. Reclaiming the land for peace, they cast seeds, planted trees and shrubs, hung pictures and banners. At one silo a white-haired grandmother climbed the fence and distributed birdseed as television and still cameras recorded the scene. At another launch site a man strolled onto the silo lid in a clown suit and tied balloons to the deadly launch instruments.

Within minutes, fourteen activists stood within the forbidden confines of ten Minuteman II launch sites. All were soon arrested.

Caught unprepared, the Air Force elected not to prosecute, deciding instead to issue letters warning offenders not to do it again.

The next day some of the participants burned their "ban and bar" letters atop another silo lid. When the Air Force again declined to prosecute, the defiance was repeated again and again.

By the end of August the federal government's reaction changed. Charges of trespass and "depredation of property" were filed first against one group of Peace Planters and then another.

By late October the first of a series of trials was underway and more prosecutions had begun. By early spring fifteen Peace Planters had been charged—the original fourteen plus one who entered a launch site in the following days. Some had been tried, convicted, and sentenced, usually to maximum terms of up to twenty-six months.

By mid-July, a year after the weekend retreat in Milwaukee, most of the Missouri Peace Planters were in prison.

Prisoners On Purpose is an outgrowth and part of Missouri Peace Planting '88. Edited, illustrated and written for the most part by the imprisoned participants in that action, the book is an attempt to broaden participation by demystifying the risks and consequences of nonviolent direct action in the cause of peace and justice.

As a peacemakers' guide to jails and prisons, the book has as its primary audience people contemplating nonviolent missile launch site entries in Missouri. It is an authoritative account of what to expect from the federal judges in Kansas City and in the local jails and regional prisons to which such offenders are likely to be committed.

To the authors of this book and their co-conspirators, that is an important target group because the issue of the morality and legality of nuclear weapons has nowhere been more starkly joined than in the Western District of Missouri, where federal prosecutors and judges practice maximum deterrence against this form of peacemaking. It is our hope, frankly, that this book will encourage the testing of that policy with growing frequency by putting useful information in the hands of those with the heart to challenge the policy.

Beyond Missouri, the lessons of the book are readily applicable to other missile silo states (North and South Dakota, Montana, Wyoming, Colorado, and Nebraska) and to any region where nuclear weapons and their systems and subsystems give local activists an opportunity to withdraw their consent. Few parts of the United States would not be included.

Like the action from which it sprang, this book is but a first step. Others who would demystify courts and prisons as part of their work for peace and justice are invited to follow this example.

Among the many who helped guide this volume through the exigencies of incarceration, the editor and contributors would like to extend special. thanks to Delany Dean, who coordinated the work from her Kansas City law office, assisted materially in the editing and contributed the chapter on what to expect in court.

Publication of this book was supported by grants from RESIST, the CS Fund, and the Peace Development Fund.

I

Challenging The Law

1

Before You Do The Action

NOT ALL THE Missouri Peace Planters were arrested and sent to jail; most members of the Peace Planter community acted as the support group. Neither this action nor any major action of direct resistance would be possible without the dedicated support of a group of people who commit themselves to be closely involved in the action from the initial planning stages until the last resister is released from jail, and beyond. Missouri Peace Planting '88 was such a community effort. It involved dozens of people, many of whom did not even know each other until they came together to make the action a reality. For some members of the Peace Planter community, personal or family circumstances prohibited the risk of jail. Others, after careful discernment, simply felt called to some role other than "going over the fence"—at least, this time.

What does it mean to be a support person?

It may mean offering hospitality in your home, overnight or for longer periods of time. Your home may take on the aura of a boarding house, with folks arriving and departing at odd hours. They will be sleeping on your couch, or maybe on your dining room floor. It's likely at least some of your guests will be vegetarians, and you'll be looking for a good recipe for meatless chili. Support may mean good long talks into the night with a pot of coffee or a jug of wine.

You'll be getting to know some new friends, and some fine and fascinating people.

Those who act as support people truly form a community together with the resisters. Of course, community does not necessarily mean that each person will become a close friend—but sometimes that does happen, and a deep love is experienced. Community means recognizing the individual, accepting the individual, and realizing that each is a special person. Community calls for honesty—trust must be built in a short time.

For some, support means going to the site of the resistance action, to witness the action, to provide transportation, to put up banners, or to take photographs. When the action is over, there are trials and sentencings to attend. Some supporters are lawyers who donate their time to give legal advice and to represent those who don't want to handle their trials alone. There are publicity chores to be done, letters to be written, and telephones to be answered. Someone has to pick up the mail and buy more stamps.

During the Missouri Peace Planting action, supporters were stationed at each missile launch site and at the nearest courthouse. They were there to provide moral support as well as to observe how the "planters" were treated by the military and law enforcement agents. Other supporters waited by telephones to receive reports from designated witnesses or an attorney verifying the whereabouts of each prisoner, to make sure no one would "fall through the cracks." These supporters acted as a safety net.

When Peace Planters were imprisoned in local county jails, supporters from the "host city" became a lifeline, providing everything from socks to postage stamps. While certain material goods were important to those imprisoned, quite often what they needed most was contact with people who cared about them, supported them, and could comfort them in their discouragement, fear, loneliness and frustration.

Nearly always, support means financial sacrifice and substantial time commitments. There are groceries to be purchased, and jails to visit. The phone bills begin to mount up, and people with jobs can get only so much vacation time and "sick" time. It's hard to find the time to write all the letters you'd like to write. But being in community means that it's possible because there will always be someone to help. Someone who hasn't much time to donate will give money, and everyone is in this together.

Support means outreach, too. When friends and family realize that your life suddenly seems to include a whole new crowd of people, people who may even be going to jail, you will be faced with questions and a fine opportunity to engage in peace education. You may even be surprised to find that the prosecutor or judge on one of the cases is a neighbor or a member of your church, and this may provide you with a splendid chance to demonstrate your solidarity with the accused by sitting with other supporters in the courtroom. Don't underestimate the power of such a witness. You will raise the level of consciousness of all those who become aware of the commitments you have made to free the earth from the specter of nuclear holocaust.

Support work also means living with the nagging feeling that you should always be doing more, more, more, yet being honest with yourself and others when you've reached your limit and know that it is time to back away for a while.

It means being stretched spiritually and morally in such a way that the oneness and interdependence of all creation starts becoming a reality. It means being challenged to take some measure of personal responsibility for the earth's fate because *never again* will you be able to plead ignorance as an excuse for doing nothing.

Some veterans say that going to jail is actually easier than doing support work. The question is debatable—perhaps the truth lies somewhere in between. The two are parts of one living organism. Supporters may need the example of those doing civil disobedience in order to be drawn further along on their own journeys. The imprisoned may need supporters to sustain them during their times of darkness, to help them maintain courage and to remind them of why they did it in the first place.

History clearly demonstrates that societal change comes not from above but from below. This means nuclear weapons will probably not be removed from our earth because one day we will elect heads of state who have sense enough to work for disarmament. But nuclear weapons must be removed from the face of the earth, and when they are removed, it will be because the consciousness of the people of this earth has awakened to the danger which confronts us all. And this awakening of consciousness will lead inevitably to such actions as Missouri Peace Planting '88. This means that each of us has an essential role to play; disarmament not only begins with us—it cannot happen without us, acting in community.

Community is essential for resistance to develop and for a new world order to be created, for it is in community that we learn about cooperation, not competition; about nonviolence as it is lived, not just as it is discussed. In our communities of resistance we confront the fact that nuclear weapons exist not only in the missile fields, but in our hearts as well. The community which gave birth to Missouri Peace Planting '88 did not do so without some painful struggles and disagreements; in the end, the greatest achievement of the community was not the climbing of fences, but the loving and respectful way in which those disputes were resolved.

Ultimately, for the individual as well as for the community, support means conversion—a change of heart and of priorities. When you become a part of a community of resistance you become, in large part, the light and hope of the planet. You have begun to reject the violence and materialism of today's society in favor of Gandhi's truth-force, the love ethic of Jesus, and the indomitable nonviolence of Martin Luther King, Jr.

2

After You Climb The Fence

THE MISSILE SILOS in Missouri are unguarded in the sense that there are no military personnel stationed at the silos, watching each one to prevent entry. There is only a fence, and not much of a fence at that. Many Peace Planters have easily climbed the fence; others have chosen to cut the flimsy lock on the gate. Once inside, sensing devices will tell personnel at the control center a few miles away that there has been an intrusion of some sort. They won't be able to tell that human beings have entered the site, only that some large object (larger than, say, a rabbit) is inside. The control center will respond by sending heavily armed military personnel to investigate, possibly in a pickup truck, maybe in an armored, tank-like vehicle known ironically as a "peacekeeper."

You will sooner or later (a few minutes or an hour or more) find yourself confronted with very young, very frightened people with automatic weapons. These Air Force security guards are trained to believe that every intrusion is hostile, and they will be extremely cautious and uptight. They will stalk around with their rifles, surround you, and order you off the site. If you go, you will go at gunpoint; if you refuse, they will carefully approach you and, if necessary, carry you off while others hold guns on you and your captor. You will probably then be searched and hand-cuffed, and you will probably find that the military folks will refuse to talk to you at all. They will wait for some civilian authority, a sheriff's deputy or highway patrol officer, to actually take you to the local county jail or sheriff's office, where you will wait to be interrogated by plainclothes Air Force detectives (members of the OSI, or Office of Special Investigations).

You will probably find that the Air Force investigators are extremely courteous and that they will interrogate you in great detail. They will probably advise you of your right to remain silent and your right to have an attorney present. If you waive or give up those rights and you decide to let them question you, you will find that they are skilled in interrogation techniques; they will be especially interested in ascertaining how the resistance action was planned and by whom; who helped you? who discussed it with you? who drove you to the site? to what organizations do you belong? how did you get to Missouri, and when? This will be their agenda, and they will resist any efforts of yours to redirect the conversation to your reasons for being there. They will, however, usually allow you to give them a written statement, in your own words, if you so desire. They will probably give you a "ban-and-bar letter" after the interrogation. In this form letter, the base commander will be issuing an order to you that you are not to reenter the property of Whiteman Air Force Base for any reason. This may be a permanent order or it may expire in a year or two.

While the interrogation is going on, there will also be a decision to be made about prosecution. An entry ("trespass") upon the site of a missile silo may be prosecuted as either a state or a federal offense. The military will probably want prosecution to occur (as opposed to just a ban-and-bar letter and a warning), but that decision is not theirs to make. It is a prosecuting attorney, the county prosecutor acting on behalf of the state, or the U.S. district attorney acting on behalf of the federal government who will decide whether prosecution is warranted. In most cases, the local county prosecutor will not be interested in prosecution, so that if the feds decline to pursue the case, you will not be brought to trial. And it may be that the U.S. attorney will delay his decision until you have been released and he can see whether or not you are going to return to the silos. If you do not return, he may decide not to prosecute. If you do return, after you have been arrested again he may ask the local jail to hold you for the U.S. marshals to come get you and put you in federal custody. The U.S. attorney may delay his decision about prosecution for quite some time, theoretically until the statute of limitations expires, in a matter of months or years.

In addition to the decision as to whether or not to prosecute, there will also be a decision made as to what charges, if any, are appropriate. If you climbed the fence and did no damage at all at the site, the only appropriate charge will be trespass, which carries a maximum penalty of six months in prison, a $500 fine, and a special assessment of $25. If, on the other hand, you destroy or damage any property, such as the lock on the gate, an additional charge of "depredation of property" may be filed, which can increase the maximum term of imprisonment to a year or more, and the fine to $1,000 or more, depending on the value of the property damaged. The more serious the damage at the site, the more likely it is that a felony charge such as sabotage or seditious conspiracy will be filed. The most serious of these charges carry possible penalties of ten or twenty years in prison, and they have been used in the past against peace activists who did substantial damage to equipment at silo sites.

If the decision has been made to prosecute while you are still in custody, the marshals will take you before a U.S. magistrate for an initial appearance. You will be advised of the charges against you, you will be asked whether you have an attorney or want one appointed for you, and your bond will be set. You may represent yourself if you wish. You will probably be allowed to make a signature bond or a bond which requires very little money, but you must promise to abide by all the conditions of bond before you will be released. Typically those conditions will require you not to go back to the silos, and to report regularly to a probation officer. If you say you will not agree to those conditions, you will be sent to a local county jail to await trial. In some cases you may be allowed to change your mind about bond, and be released later, or to go into jail if you have been released. Any time you serve in jail before trial will be credited to you against any sentence you may be ordered to serve.

Typically a trial will occur two or three months after the charges are filed. If charges are not filed until after you have been released, you will be notified and asked to voluntarily surrender yourself so that you can be brought to trial. If you do not agree to do this, a warrant will be issued for your arrest.

The trial may take on one of several different forms, depending on the whim of the presiding judge. You may or may not be denied a jury; you may or may not be allowed to present evidence as to international law, nuclear weapons, or your personal religious or moral reasons for having gone to the silo. If you testify at your trial, you may be asked questions about who helped you to plan or execute the action; if you refuse to answer, you may be held in contempt and assessed additional time (up to six months for each contempt). You may be tried alone or with other defendants. The trial will consist primarily of testimony by Air Force personnel who will testify that the property belongs to the Air Force, that there are signs on the fences announcing that trespassing is forbidden, and that they saw you there on the day charged. You or your lawyer may cross-examine these witnesses. You may call witnesses and testify yourself, but typically the judge will order you not to put on any evidence or testimony about matters he considers irrelevant, i.e., international law, the necessity defense, your real reasons for going to the silo. The trial will usually last one or two days.

After the trial, if you are found guilty, the judge will order a presentence investigation. This begins with a lengthy interview between you and a probation officer; the interview and the investigation are intended to produce an informative report for the sentencing judge to assist him in deciding what sentence to give you. Your family and friends and employers may be contacted; your financial resources will be investigated. This process may take a couple of months.

After the presentence report is complete, you will be given a sentencing date. At the actual sentencing, you will be given an opportunity to address the court, and the court, i.e., the judge, will of course have an opportunity to address *you*, typically to explain how misguided he believes you are, and to explain why he feels it necessary to give you a harsh sentence. He may offer you probation instead of jail but, as with pretrial release on bond, probation carries certain conditions (perhaps a form of house arrest at a local halfway house as well as a promise not to go back to the silos) and it lasts two or three years. Sentencing for Peace Planters in the Western District of Missouri has been very harsh. People who only entered silos on one occasion, and who voluntarily surrendered themselves for prosecution, have been sentenced to the maximum term of six months. People who went back repeatedly have also been given maximum or near maximum terms, some up to two years. In past years, peace activists who have entered missile silos and damaged equipment or silo lids have received sentences of up to eighteen years.

Under new federal sentencing statutes, there is no good time (time off for "good behavior") for any sentence under one year. Good time is earned at the rate of fifty-four days annually after completion of the first full year.

The judge will also decide at the sentencing whether to allow you "voluntary surrender," i.e., a chance to go home after the sentencing, wait to be notified of the institution at which your sentence will be served, and then just drive up to the gate and surrender. It may be possible to be granted this option even if you are not on bond at the time of sentencing; on the other hand, many who were on bond were denied this privilege and taken into custody at the sentencing.

The actual sentences are typically, but not universally, served at minimum security federal prisons or camps. The decision as to where you will serve your sentence is made by the Bureau of Prisons (BOP). After the sentencing, the BOP evaluates the individual in terms of prior history of criminal convictions, severity of the present offense, and length of sentence.

They also consider any request which you have made for a particular institution, as well as any recommendation by the judge; and they do make some effort to place people in institutions near their homes. They then designate the institution and notify the marshals that you are to be transported to that location. Their policy is to keep the designated location a secret, at least until you are en route. Sometimes the marshals will tell you in advance where you are going, but you can't count on that. Just rest assured that, in two or three weeks after the sentence is pronounced, you will be "disappeared," and your travel odyssey to your designated institution will begin.

II

County Jails

3

Cass County Women's Jail

THE CASS COUNTY JAIL, in Harrisonville, Missouri, is a sort of Grand Central Station for women silo resisters in Missouri. No matter where your train is eventually headed, it most likely starts here.

In keeping with that, the place is very public. The gals live elbow to elbow in one large room—capacity twelve. You can get to know people pretty well when you spend twenty-four hours a day in the same box with them.

Privacy can be had in the shower stall.

There are six bunks, one long metal table with metal benches on either side, one camera to monitor your every move, one sink, one shower, one toilet. One TV. One hot water pot. One chowhatch. One double-lock entry/exit passage.

The twelfth bunk, top side next to the shower stall, is warped and makes a noise like thunder if you move around.

The color to keep in mind here is grey. The bars are grey, the concrete floor is grey, the table, sink, toilet, shower are all grey metal, the walls are grey cement block. There is no view of the outside world. Fluorescent lights glare at you twenty-four hours a day. There is an ongoing tussle between the women, who put up blankets to block out the light, and the guards, who order the blankets down.

The air is also grey—with smoke. There is a ventilator which runs twice a day. Other than that you get recycled cigarette smoke from people who do this sort of thing all day long. There seems to be a high percentage of them in the population here.

The noise level is also high. There is no noise curfew, and quite often people will be up, and loud, all night long. If sleep is what you need, good luck. Maybe you can take a nap tomorrow. Like the guard says, if it was fun, everyone would want to stay here.

Women are allowed outside the cell only for visits, medical appointments, and, on rare occasions, for thirty minutes of recreation in a gravel-covered lot (about the size of the concrete lid on a Missouri nuclear missile silo). Indoor recreation is limited to card playing, board games, art work with pens and crayons, reading, and calisthenics. There are no cubicles or dividers in this crowded place. Every motion or sound you make is seen and heard by all. On the men's side, prisoners can retreat into two-person cells at night to sleep, or in the day to talk. The women have no such privilege.

Afternoon and evening meals, prepared in the kitchen of a defunct restaurant, enter the bullpen through "the chowhatch" on plastic trays. The food is boring, bland, overcooked, and not terribly nutritious. Vegetarians may have a hard time of it. The main dish for lunch and dinner is usually "mystery meat." You can supplement your diet with junk food from the commissary. The morning fare, one box of cereal and one carton of milk, is placed on the cell bars at about 6 a.m. Cleaning supplies and some personal hygiene items are also passed in through the bars, but quite irregularly.

There are no lockers or other storage units in the cell. Belongings get stashed underneath bottom bunks, between the bars, or under your mattress. Jail bars make good bookcases.

The shower has no knobs, only a button which, when pressed, dispenses one temperature of water for about thirty seconds; then, it must be pressed again.

Unlike the males, who must pound on the windows to gain the guards' attention, women shout their needs into an intercom box. If guards feel vexed or overburdened, they switch off the intercom. Even when the device is turned on, responses are sporadic to requests for items such as toilet paper, sanitary napkins, paper towels, aspirin, and cleaning supplies.

Processing of new arrivals can take several hours, because a single guard does the paperwork (in triplicate), photos, fingerprints, strip searches, and spraying for lice. You wait in a one-person holding cell, grey concrete with bars, a metal bunk, and a toilet, while the men go first. After you've been given a jail uniform—possibly a yellow-orange sweatsuit with pants that are too big around the waist—you are finally escorted to the women's side.

Women are each issued two sweatsuits upon arrival. White underwear, socks, and T-shirts may be sent in. Two women prisoners are selected, on the basis of seniority, to launder clothing, towels, and bedding for the entire institution. Friendship with the laundry workers is advantageous.

Also allowed in from the outside are writing materials, books, and newspapers. Cass County Jail prisoners are not required to work, which leaves many hours to read, write, and study. Some find that earplugs or radio headphones enhance concentration amid the noise and distractions.

You'll find that your sleeping schedule shifts while you're here. Most folks get up shortly before lunch at 11:30 and retire at 3 a.m. or 4. The mattresses, while thin, are comfortable. It's good exercise to swing up and down to the top bunk, so don't pass it by; it may be the only exercise you get!

Outside friends may not send food items, presumably because imports might interfere with commissary sales. Snack food items, some personal hygiene supplies, and cigarettes may be purchased weekly from the commissary. Outside friends can also deposit funds in one's account.

Medicine is delivered three times a day, by prescription of a doctor—*their* doctor. It is better not to get sick, however. If one person, even a guard, brings in cold or flu germs, everyone in the cell is apt to catch it, and as people are released and new folks check in, the disease hangs around for weeks. Medical treatment leaves much to be desired.

A camera lens installed on the wall opposite the shower and commode is used by guards to monitor women prisoners. Late nights and early mornings are prime viewing hours for the guards. Sometimes they joke about what they see. A large table, turned upright, stands before the shower and commode, giving some measure of privacy. Guards and trusties generally announce themselves before approaching the barred walls by shouting, "La-dees, are ya' decent?" Guards appear at fairly predictable intervals to pass out medication, meals, and, later in the evening, the day's mail. Outgoing mail is picked up each weekday and may be sealed. Incoming mail is opened and inspected for contraband.

Access to the phone, located inside the cell, is relatively easy, since at most only thirteen people compete to use it. The phone is removed, however, whenever federal marshals are transporting any Cass County Jail prisoners to or from the Federal Court Building.

Conflicts within the cell rise in proportion to the number of occupants. When the population reaches the maximum, tensions escalate significantly. Even the most hospitable "old-timer" is likely to wince at word of a new arrival, since newcomers inevitably encroach on the already minimal

available space. Departures are often followed by a sigh of relief as occupants adjust to more elbow space and perhaps even a little more storage space, using empty bunks.

The upside of this packed-in living arrangement is that there's so much interaction. Seldom will you get another chance to meet so many women on such an intimate basis, and so involuntarily. For the most part the ladies rise to the occasion and practice courtesy with each other. Not always.

But always there will be laughter. The absurdity of being locked up in this cage, coupled incongruously with the easy small-town attitude of the jailers, breeds a sitcom kind of atmosphere, where the lines come fast and funny. They can box you in, but they can't stop you from laughing.

The guards are even likely to laugh with you. They're pretty nice for the most part, and quite willing to deliver phone messages or run errands when they can.

Most often, women at the Cass County Jail face federal drug charges and are awaiting trials, sentencing, or transport. One can expect to be regaled, fascinated, and moved by the stories they share.

All new arrivals, male and female, are booked and photographed just outside the bullpen, so women maintain an ongoing "who's who" of the Cass County Jail prison population. One 2 a.m. arrival, quite inebriated, was booked on a charge of beating his wife. "Well, ain't this a helluva thing," he shouted, not realizing that two peaceniks had been jailed ahead of him. "They lets these missile silo sitters go scot free, and they pull me outa' my own home for no reason at all."

(Note: in mid-1989 the women were moved into two cell blocks formerly occupied by men, evidently in response to complaints of sex discrimination. At the same time, some of the women's privileges were revoked.)

4

Cass County Men's Jail

THE MALE SECTION of the Cass County Jail is relatively new and incorporates the "pod" design prevalent in contemporary jail architecture. Unlike the older cell block layout, where cells with steel bars and manual locks are aligned in rows or "alleys," the pod design employs plexiglass and electronic locks. Here, four cell blocks or "tanks" form a semicircle around the control room hub. They can house seventy-five to eighty men. Both inmates and control room staff can be observed through large plexiglass windows. Visit any modern zoo which has dispensed with bars in favor of glass and you'll get the picture. It's like the Great Ape House in Chicago's Lincoln Park Zoo—though the primates undoubtedly receive better care.

The jail's four cell blocks for male prisoners vary in capacity from sixteen to twenty-four men. "D" Block is reserved for federal prisoners to segregate them from the county prisoners in the other three blocks. Inmates are billeted in pairs in cramped cells fitted with a metal sink, mirror, steel toilet (no seat), and metal bunk beds. The mattresses are two inches thick and hard as boards; the pillows look and feel like sacks of mortar. Prisoners are locked in from midnight to 6 a.m. on weeknights. The cells are stacked in two tiers (six cells to a tier). They open into a common area (or "bullpen") with four steel picnic tables for eating and card playing, and a single-faucet shower room. A television set and a pot for heating hot water also are available. Each tank also has a telephone (outgoing collect calls only) which is shut off shortly before and during inmate transfers by U.S. marshals.

The jail provides each inmate with soap, a toothbrush, toothpaste, a comb, a towel, two sheets, a blanket, and a two-piece uniform. Underwear, socks, and T-shirts (in limited quantities) may be dropped off on Sundays by outside support people. Other than underwear, personal clothing is not permitted in the jail. Court clothes are secured in nonaccessible lockers. Sometimes the guards will forget to retrieve all your clothes after a court visit—don't offer to give everything back. Having a few personal clothing items can provide a sense of normalcy.

The jail is run by a surly Vietnam vet named Major Nicholson (Nick). If you need anything special he's the man to see.

The Cass County Jail gets good grades on three counts: (1) it is clean (no roaches!); (2) the telephone access is adequate, especially during the day; and (3) the jail provides laundry service. In typical sexist fashion, women inmates are required to do the laundry.

But it gets a failing grade in the matter of outdoor recreation. The jail has a tiny outdoor exercise yard with a gravel surface and a single basketball hoop. No other recreation equipment is available. It provides an inmate's only access to fresh air and sunshine—but don't count on spending much time there. You'll get to the yard once a week if you're lucky, once a month if you're not. The jail has no library but allows visitors to drop off paperback books, portable radio/tape players, and cassette tapes. Batteries, food, and other personal hygiene items are available once a week from the commissary service. Inmates expecting federal incarceration should remember that *all* personal belongings will be shipped home (at the government's expense) when you hit the first federal prison. The food is unremarkable. Meals are served on trays by inmate trusties and eaten in the tank. Breakfast consists of two small cartons of milk and a small box of cereal. Lunch and dinner are usually hot meals. No consideration is made for vegetarian or other special diets. Unless you have money on your commissary account ("on your books"), count on losing weight. Visits are limited to two fifteen-minute sessions per week (glass and telephone). The jail will relay telephone messages to inmates, which greatly facilitates contact with the outside world. Guard harassment of inmates is minimal.

Medical care is limited to a weekly visit by a pill-pushing doctor or a nurse.

The noise in the tank is deafening and the smoke suffocating. Because most of the inmates are young and awaiting trial or sentencing, tension is high. Most of the federal inmates here are black American and Jamaican, facing long prison sentences for drug-related offenses. Despite the tight quarters and the stress, physical violence is rare. By sticking to yourself you can avoid most problems. Cigarettes are the coin of the realm in jail—always have a pack on hand to repay favors. Generally, co-defendants can meet face-to-face during attorney visits. Communication with guards is more cumbersome. You get their attention by pounding on the glass like an ill-mannered primate until one of them responds over the intercom.

If you decide to refuse bond prior to trial, count on having no legal resources for pretrial preparation unless your lawyer supplies them. The jail has no law library and it is difficult to arrange a visit to the law library in the Kansas City federal courthouse. An electric typewriter is available.

Although nonviolent activists are almost always freed on bond if they wish, county jail time is nevertheless still worth considering. The experience is good "basic training" for federal prison. If you can do thirty days in a county jail, you can do a year in a federal correctional institution or prison camp with no problem (and you'll be credited for the jail time). More importantly, doing the "hard time" in a county jail will forever sensitize you to the psychological hardships of enforced idleness inflicted on county inmates. In an FCI or camp, you have access to open space and recreation programs.

The dungeon-like county jail can be a monastic experience, a journey into deeper spirituality and self-awareness. But it is also a crucible in which your tolerance and patience will be severely tested.

5

Lafayette County Jail

THE LAFAYETTE COUNTY Jail in Lexington, Missouri, about fifty miles east of Kansas City, holds up to eighty prisoners in four cell blocks—separate "communities" in which prisoners eat, sleep, and pass the time. The basic living unit is the cell, a metal and concrete cage fitted with four double-decker bunks, a toilet bowl, and wash basin.

Prisoners sleep in their cells but are allowed out in the daytime and evening for meals, showers, and television in a common room, called a "bullpen," at the front of each cell block. Food is passed into the bullpen on paper and plastic plates and eaten at a long metal table. Each cell block is provided regularly with such necessities as plastic utensils, toilet paper, bathing soap, soap flakes and detergent for laundry, and brooms and mops for housecleaning. In addition each prisoner is issued a mattress, blanket, and bright orange coveralls with black letters on the back identifying the wearer as an inmate of the LAF CO JAIL.

Your movements as a prisoner are strictly controlled. Whether in your cell, the bullpen, or a nearby recreation room, you are always locked in. The recreation room consists of a ping-pong table, small basketball court, and a single telephone. Access to the recreation room is limited by the fact that it must be shared by all four cell blocks and because it also serves as the visiting room. It is available for recreation and phone calls a maximum of three times a week.

Population of the jail varies from time to time. Often a cell will have one or two bunks vacant, in which case the empty bunks become storage shelves for food, books, magazines, and electric heating pots brought in by visitors or mailed to prisoners. The jail's policy on what may be sent in is quite liberal. The general rule is that any food is acceptable if it arrives unopened from the store. Most cell grocery shelves are loaded with candy, cookies, potato chips, and other junk food. Lafayette County also allows prisoners to keep money, watches, and other valuables—a departure from the policy of most jails. Inspections for contraband are few and far between.

In general, the jail policy is "live and let live," reflecting the style and personality of the sheriff, Eugene Darnell, who is short-tempered and cantankerous but runs a loose ship. The guards seldom hassle the prisoners, and vice versa. Prisoners and guards are on a first-name basis. For prisoners willing and able to pay, guards fetch Pepsi-Cola from the pop machine once or twice a day and send out for pizza and fried chicken on weekend evenings. Particularly notable is the attentiveness of Paula, the jail "mother," who on weekdays serves the food, brings the mail, cashes money orders, washes towels and blankets, fetches medicines and pills, and performs countless other errands for the prisoners. She is universally liked and respected.

The food is nourishing but dull, the menu highly predictable. Breakfast consists of biscuits and gravy on Monday, cold cereal on Tuesday and Thursday, scrambled eggs on Wednesday, and pancakes with syrup on Friday (no breakfast on weekends). Supper consists invariably of two sandwiches and two Oreo cookies, occasionally supplemented by an orange or banana. Hot meals are always served at noon: a heaping plate of meat, vegetable, and dessert, topped with two slices of white bread.

Prisoners here are of all kinds and types—from the occasional nonviolent peace activist to the not-so-occasional big-time drug dealer on his way to a forty-year term in the federal penitentiary. Some of the toughest and most volatile of the inmates are youngsters in their teens or early twenties brought here on such charges as burglary and robbery. They have high energy and low frustration levels, and they are prone to feuding and fighting. Disturbances of one kind or another, sometimes provoked by irrational or inconsistent jail policies, are frequent in this place. The sheriff does not hesitate to put them down with mace. The mature prisoner can minimize hazard to himself (or herself, except that no women prisoners are sent here) by steering clear of cliques, feuds, and factions. As in other jails, there are opportunities here for meeting and forming close bonds with interesting people from many walks of life. The nightly card games are a good way to get acquainted. The jail also affords splendid opportunities for reading and writing. Try to get a bunk with a good light.

As in any jail, the noise, tobacco smoke, and crowded conditions are bothersome at first. But you'll get used to these after a while. The time will go quickly if you establish a work schedule of reading and writing. The most frustrating part of being in jail is its restriction of your contact with friends and loved ones. Visits are limited to thirty minutes with one or two people once a week—by telephone through a window of the recreation room. As for long-distance telephoning—theoretically you have a crack at it three times a week, but sometimes, for one reason or another (either a prisoner faction hogs the phone or the sheriff shuts down the recreation room for disciplinary reasons), weeks may go by without your getting to the telephone. The solution to the problem: be thankful for the occasional visit and phone conversation, but depend on the mail for maintaining and strengthening your ties with the outside world. No typewriter or lap-top word processors available here—just a pen, a writing pad, a metal bunk, and a light bulb protruding from the wall. You'll be astounded to discover how well, after all these years, the ancient art of letter writing still serves to spread the word.

6

St. Clair County Jail

THE ST. CLAIR COUNTY JAIL opened in 1988 in Osceola, Missouri, a small town about a hundred miles south of Kansas City. You'll find it between missile silos G-4 and G-5.

The jail holds about forty inmates, most of whom are apt to be federal prisoners convicted of drug-related offenses. Each cell is fitted with two, three, or four metal bunks bolted to the walls, a shelf and reading light, sink with hot and cold water, mirror, toilet, fluorescent lighting, and electrical outlets. Some people use the outlets for boom boxes. The only bars in this plexiglass prison are inside the opaque glass windows of the cell blocks. Air conditioning keeps the temperature pleasant all year 'round.

At 6 a.m. each morning a guard opens the doors to a breakfast of cold cereal, milk, juice, and sometimes an orange. Lunch and supper, usually hot and good, come in styrofoam boxes and cups. The apple pie gets high marks. For those who object to the usual highly processed, institutional meat, the jail has been known to replace it with egg and cheese sandwiches and salad. Meals are eaten on two tables in a day room which also includes a television set and a single shower for up to ten prisoners.

Guards run the jail from a plexiglass-enclosed control center from which doors can be electronically opened. A pay phone is available two days a week, or oftener, and calls to lawyers can be arranged any time.

When you are booked in you will be given a handbook of rules and information, such as "prisoners without funds may request materials and postage for up to three letters per week." Then you will be taken to a shower room to be sprayed with bug killer and given a shower. You will be issued sheets, blanket, pillow, and mattress (usually plastic covered). Prisoners wear their own clothing, which is washed along with bedding once a week. It's a good idea to mark your underclothes for identification.

Prisoners while away the time with cards, dominoes, body-building, and push-ups. They play basketball in a small courtyard with a screened-in skylight providing inmates their only fresh air and sunlight.

Prisoners are allowed daily visits from 6 to 8 p.m. on Monday through Thursday and 1 to 4 p.m. on Friday through Sunday. Visitors can stay up to forty-five minutes if time permits. They must show photo identification.

Food cannot be brought into the jail, but it may be ordered from the commissary once a week along with toiletries, batteries, and writing materials. A fundamentalist evangelical preacher from the Bible Baptist Church in Osceola visits the jail on Tuesday evenings. Attending the service may be your only chance to meet a friend from another cell block.

Being a prisoner in the St. Clair County Jail is like being in a shelter for the homeless. The guards give you the same feeling of helplessness. But rather than scaring you, jail experience is more likely to take away your fear.

III

Federal Prisons

7

Getting There

IF YOU HAVE BEEN SENTENCED to prison by a federal court, and if the judge will allow it, you will save yourself a lot of hassle by arranging for "self-surrender" in which you report to a given institution at a given time. That way you'll bypass the discomforts of confinement in a local jail and transportation as a federal prisoner. On the other hand, if you're interested in new experiences, there's nothing quite so novel as riding to prison as a guest of Uncle Sam.

First, get used to the idea of being bound hand and foot. Everywhere you travel you'll be clapped in hand-cuffs connected to a chain around your waist and ankle cuffs connected by a chain just long enough to permit you to hobble in and out of vehicles and airplanes.

Federal marshals will transport you in chains from the courthouse to the county jail in an automobile or van fitted with a cage-like iron screen, making you feel a little like a mad dog being taken to the pound.

Cars, vans, and prison buses are also sometimes used for longer trips lasting up to a day or two. In that case you'll be given sandwiches at mealtime and lodged overnight in a local jail or federal institution. Toilet facilities are in the back of the bus—and good luck to you in getting the job done while handcuffed!

Increasingly, however, the Bureau of Prisons uses its "airlift" to move inmates from institution to institution around the country. The airlift consists of two Boeing 727s capable of seating about 140 each. Staffed by federal marshals dressed in blue jump suits, they are in service from dawn until early evening, with time out only for maintenance and repairs.

A typical day on the airlift might begin at 2 in the morning, when you are roused from sleep at the Federal Correctional Institution at El Reno, Oklahoma (for men), or the local jail at Norman, Oklahoma (for women), the institutions that serve as the central states hub of the prison transportation system.

Led to a bullpen with other prisoners bound for distant places, you are strip-searched, reclothed, fed, manacled, and driven by prison bus to a remote corner of the Oklahoma City airport, where you are met by a squad of marshals at parade rest, shotguns cocked on their hips and pointed skyward. It is an impressive sight.

Your bus pulls up behind the plane, a big craft with no markings to identify its unique function. Alighting from the bus, you are checked off by name, prison number, and mug shot (from a sheaf of papers held by a marshal who alone may know your destination), patted down, then directed up the tail ramp, and shown to your seat by one of the jump suits.

Seatbelts? Most prisoners ignore them and few marshals seem to care whether you wear them. But, with persistence, you can manage to snap them tight despite your handcuffs.

Need to take a pee? Lots of luck. A marshal will keep a watchful eye on you, the toilet door open, as your handcuffed fingers struggle with pants and underpants.

The plane may make as many as a dozen stops during the long day, picking up prisoners and disgorging others in widely scattered parts of the country before returning to its Oklahoma City home. If you're still aboard at lunchtime you may receive a cheap frozen meal—probably still frozen. Somewhere along

the line you'll be deposited on the backstretch of some airport or air base, there to be met by shotgun-toting marshals who will herd you into a car bound for some jail or prison nearby or still far away.

In addition to a stay of indeterminate length at El Reno or Norman, your prison term can also include a sojourn as a "holdover" in some local jail or federal institution. These layovers can sometimes last a week or more.

One such temporary resting place is the U.S. Penitentiary at Leavenworth, Kansas, where the holdover unit also serves as the disciplinary segregation unit, or "hole," for the nearby Leavenworth Prison Camp. Located within the walls of the huge, forbidding penitentiary, the hole is a locked dormitory room with bunks for fifteen or twenty. The food is good and the place is clean, but the close confinement makes this an onerous cage. You are locked in the room around the clock except for daily one-hour trips (with wrists handcuffed behind your back) to the exercise yard or the TV room.

Transportation can be the most difficult part of your prison experience not only because of the restraints and close confinement but also because you are in limbo, out of touch with friends and loved ones. Phone opportunities are rare, mail takes a long time catching up with you, and the prisoners with whom you come in contact are strangers.

Movement from your place of initial confinement to your ultimate prison destination usually takes only a day or two, but longer trips of up to ten days or two weeks are not unusual. Sometimes, usually for disciplinary reasons, the trip from jail to jail can become an aimless, endless journey lasting months. Prisoners call this "diesel therapy."

8

Norman And El Reno

FOR INMATES ENTERING the federal prison system in the central United States, most roads lead through Oklahoma—a central terminal for the Bureau of Prisons airlift.

Women destined for prisons all over the country are housed in the Cleveland County Detention Center (CCDC) at Norman, near Oklahoma City. Men are lodged for a night, a week, or sometimes a month in a special section of the federal prison at El Reno, about thirty miles to the west.

The women who shuffle in shackles into the CCDC are fingerprinted, interviewed, strip-searched, and fed. The meal, while primitive, is bound to be better than the food which was provided on the plane. The strip search is the "bend over and spread your cheeks" variety.

All clothing except underwear and bra are taken away and replaced by an orange canvas dress and loafer gym shoes. Decked out in such apparel, you will grab a roll containing a towel, unclean sheet, a blanket, a mat, and maybe a toothbrush and toothpaste. You will *not* be provided with shampoo, comb, pillow, or drinking cup; and you may not get any soap, either.

The one orange dress will have to do you for a week, when, if you're still here, you'll get a clean one on laundry day. If you wear a white T-shirt and a couple of pairs of socks and underwear in transit, you'll be able to wash out one set and wear the other.

The steel and cement cell block at Norman holds two floors of cells—seven on top, six on the bottom—opening into a large day room. The day room houses a few uncomfortable chairs; women carry rolled-up blankets to protect their bottoms. A small black and white TV set perches on an overturned waste can near the one telephone. The inmates share a single shower room that has two showerheads.

Each cell has two bunks, a metal toilet, a sink, and a window; when the noise in the dayroom gets to you, you can retreat into your cell to read or take a nap. At 11 p.m. all inmates are locked down in their cells. You'll find the metal bunk and thin mattress are more comfortable than they look. After a little while the lights go out automatically; they come back on at 7 in the morning, and breakfast is half an hour later.

Big brother lurks big time in CCDC. Communication with the guards is over an intercom in each cell. The doors lock and unlock, open and close by remote control. Faceless guards maintain security by means of one-way glass and cameras. Requests for sanitary napkins, toilet paper, and other personal supplies, conveyed by intercom, can take hours to satisfy.

As a federal prisoner in transit, you will probably not be there long enough to set up a commissary account. So you'll only receive two free stamps a week, and other supplies, such as pencil, paper, envelopes, comb, shampoo, deodorant, must be borrowed from "state girls"—women who are serving time or awaiting legal proceedings in Cleveland County—or done without. The outnumbered state women are understandably reluctant to let the ever-changing cast of federal women borrow from them.

Sanitary napkins are doled out one at a time. Hair ties and barrettes are not allowed. Every night there is a long wait to use the phone. Paperbacks, cards, and TV are the only diversions. The place is noisy; the shower is too hot or too cold. You won't be told you are leaving until very early on the morning of your departure.

The harsh environment, the forced deprivation, the rivalry with local women, and the uncertainty of departure date, all combine to create a constant state of tension. But friendships bloom and fade, and opportunities for conversation are plentiful.

Typical of the men's dormitories at El Reno FCI is Oklahoma II, which houses up to forty transients who may be held there up to a month. Bunk beds fill the room, and sometimes cots are added. There are showers. A cable television set is mounted atop shelves of used books. Bibles are plentiful. Another shelf holds chess, checkers, dominoes, jigsaw puzzles, and other games. A guard issues toothbrushes, brushing powder, comb, and towel. A telephone is available.

Food is of greater quantity and quality at El Reno than at most county jails. After supper, prisoners usually spend about an hour in a small grassy area that has a couple of tables and trees.

Holdovers at El Reno, just as at Norman, usually have no access to the commissary. Smokers are at the mercy of the guards, some of whom may give a cigarette or two as pay for such chores as sweeping the floor. Inmates are given free writing paper, pencils, and envelopes, but only three stamps are issued weekly, on Wednesday. You'll have to borrow or beg more from fellow inmates.

Prisoners are counted several times a day at El Reno. On the weekends the TV stays on til 1 a.m., but the lights are turned out at 10:30 p.m., making it impossible to read or write, difficult to sleep, and a good time to watch a movie with the boys. On Sunday there are Protestant and Catholic worship services in a large, stone church in the yard.

There's also a chance you'll be housed in the seg-regation unit during your stay at El Reno. In that case, you'll be locked in a two-man cell most of the time, with one telephone call a week and outdoor excercise once or twice a week.

After a few days of life as a holdover in Oklahoma, you'll be ready for the marshals and the shackles, and a trip to someplace which should be considerably better than Norman or El Reno.

9

Lexington

TO IMAGINE the Lexington Federal Correctional Institution at Lexington, Kentucky, where 1,300 to 1,350 women are confined, think of the red brick walls and cream-colored tiles of your old high school. Then add a razor wire fence.

Most of the prisoners live in a cluster of three-story dorms—called Bluegrass, Numen, and Antaeus—overlooking a small courtyard called Central Park, which also adjoins two other buildings, one for administrative offices and the other containing dining halls, a hospital, the library, game rooms, and three additional dorms.

Corridor guards exercise "crowd control" by preventing conversations and by checking for passes. "They only know five sentences," says an inmate, "'No talking!,' 'La-dees, clear the halls!,' 'Lemme see your pass,' 'What do you have in that bag?,' and 'Counting!'"

New arrivals are outfitted with a couple of changes of underwear and socks, khaki apparel, which is sturdy and comfortable, and steel-toed shoes. Lexington limits clothing packages from the outside to one box of approved apparel per year.

Commissary shortages make weekly "shopping" trips frustrating because personal items are sometimes removed or placed on the "out" list. On one occasion no deodorant was available for two weeks. Removal of hair dyes and certain perm kits raised quite a stir. After a random locker search guards confiscated blow driers and curling irons which the commissary had sold to women, and then simply threw them out, saying that those products were contraband.

Particularly irksome to some is the institution's refusal to sell envelopes at the commissary, requiring prisoners to ask residence hall officials for envelopes. These requests meet with varying success. Some women say that one of the main advantages of participating in the institution's PACT program (Parents and Children Together) is that you get to use tape and paper to fabricate your own envelopes. (Incidentally, few women actually have much time together with their children while incarcerated at Lexington.)

Why does Lexington have more stringent regulations than other penal institutions for women? Partly it's because the Bureau of Prisons' main medical facilities for women are there. The institution must be able to accommodate sick prisoners of all but the highest security levels. So all inmates are subjected to regulations deemed appropriate for the higher security levels. Mixing of security levels has been an issue of intense concern for many women imprisoned there. Some fear for their safety and many who have lower security levels protest subjection to more stringent rules intended for people who have committed more serious crimes. But should women of a higher security level be isolated from other prisoners? Some women with lower security levels have access to supportive networks outside the walls and thus are in a position to go to bat for incarcerated women of all levels.

If a woman's presentence investigation suggests possible health complications or need for medical treatment, she will very likely be designated to Lexington—and kept there if her sentence has less than a year to run.

The overcrowding at Lexington is awesome. Imagine the longest grocery store lines you've ever waited in; imagine public transportation during Christmas rush in busy cities; those images will offer some idea of what daily lines are like in the cafeteria, at sick call, at the commissary, at the stamp and coin machines, for pill distribution, for phone use, and at recreational events.

Many women sleep in bunks wedged into spaces that once served as TV lounges, card playing rooms, even storage rooms. In one of the least crowded dormitories, Mary Todd, five women share a relatively spacious room furnished with two double-decker bunks, one single bed, five lockers (again reminiscent of high school), and five metal chairs. In some of the more crowded dorms, up to seventy-five women may share one bathroom and only two showers. At one time, the 250 to 300 residents of Numen Unit had access to only one operable washer and drier.

Meals are adequate, although quite high in starches and carbohydrates. Vegetarians can usually find nourishment at the salad bar, which is open during lunch and dinner. The dining halls are nearly always overcrowded during lunch and dinner, making it difficult to sit with friends. Guards circulate between the tables, and are quick to instruct you to leave as soon as your plate is emptied. Long lines form not only to enter the cafeteria but also to deposit trays, and sometimes women must wait in line to be frisked before leaving the dining hall.

Case managers and counselors generally appear overburdened with fifty to 100 people on their caseloads. An urge to avoid additional paperwork may explain the abrupt and aloof manner which characterizes most of the staff's interactions with women prisoners here. Approval of visiting lists and receipt of boxes from the outside must be secured through your counselor, along with any desired changes in work assignments.

Visitors are allowed on weekend days and during three weeknights. Immediate family members are automatically allowed as visitors. By submitting names and addresses of no more than six friends to your counselor, you can initiate the process of getting approval for nonfamily visits. This process can take as long as two months.

Visiting takes place in a large, linoleum-tiled room, full of small plastic tables and plastic chairs. Visitors should bring change to feed the vending machines which supply the only available food.

On one weekend of each month, mothers and children are allowed to go to a PACT playroom for two hours. When the PACT room is not open, children can play in a small TV room, with a meager assortment of toys. Separations between mothers and children at the end of visiting hours are bleak and tearful experiences.

All prisoners are required to work in some capacity. Pay rates range from $5 per month for menial and unskilled labor to $1.40 per hour for some prison industry jobs. Refusal to work would probably result in a transfer to the hole.

Outdoors, Lexington has its charms. Miles of fields stretch beyond the fence, affording an occasional glimpse of grazing horses. In the Big Yard, various ethnic groups can be seen dancing to their favorite music. Clusters of people gather around picnic tables and the more energetic jog or walk briskly around a huge track. Plenty of sports equipment is available, including a quaint but inoperable miniature golf course.

There are other ways to escape the prison tedium. The Spanish and Gospel choirs practice almost every night, giving members a strong sense of community. Rich textures and creative expressions in the art studio and craft room offer respite from the gleaming sterility of the institution. The library, fairly well stocked and carpeted, is an oasis of relative calm. Those wishing to learn Spanish may find excellent opportunities for learning through "immersion" in the language.

Most women at Lexington are there for drug-related crimes. Contrary to "war on drugs" rhetoric, most of these women interact nonviolently, even under stress.

A sojourn in Lexington can introduce you to a variety of cultures and classes. It can expose you to dramatic life stories. It can help you transcend barriers of age, class, nation, and race.

10

Alderson

ALDERSON FCI, a "federal correctional institution" for women, has been designated as a "camp" by the Federal Bureau of Prisons. It nestles in the West Virginia foothills, far from the noise and congestion of any city.

All of middle America might benefit from this kind of camping experience. It isn't difficult to gain admittance. Some applicants qualify by reconstructing military installations, some plant corn and flowers and insist on hanging banners, and some just sit and pray on top of nuclear missile silos. But whatever your means of entering, once you're in camp your education begins.

The first step upon arrival is orientation. It is helpful to pretend you are "Alice in Wonderland." You'll be presented with a booklet describing all the "no-no's" and what's contraband. Chewing gum is a *real* no-no, and such innocuous items as brown paper or plastic bags if found in your locker or on your person can get you extra duty or a few days in the hole.

The hole is where you go for breaking the rules. You may stay there a few days or a few months, depending on the "crime." Or you can be shipped out. Activities there will be limited to reading, writing, sleeping, and eating, with one hour of recreation per day.

Built to accommodate 400 to 450 women, Alderson now houses 800 to 900. The buildings into which these prisoners are crowded sprawl across the rolling hills in what looks like an apartment complex or a small private college. People refer to the grounds as the "campus." But appearances can be deceiving.

Seniority and good behavior determine where you'll live—a dormitory for six or twelve, a double or single room. It takes eight months to a year of good conduct to earn a single room. The dormitories are called "cottages," but don't let the term confuse you. Approximately seventy-five women live in each building. "Honor cottages" house only half that many— but they say qualifying for admittance is tougher than winning the Congressional Medal of Honor.

Other buildings house the visiting and recreation rooms, dining hall, prison factories, power house, and other facilities. There is a lot of walking space among the trees and fields.

Prisoners are expected to work. If you choose not to work you can expect a trip to the hole and transfer to some other institution.

Movement is relatively unrestricted here. You'll be required to sign in and out of your dorm so the authorities can keep track of you.

For recreation you'll have films, pool, indoor and outdoor sports, limited bicycle riding, table games, crafts, ceramics, religious activities, card games, a small library, and, naturally, television. Sometimes there is entertainment from the outside. On one occasion inmates watched a baseball game between male staff members and a local church team. It was unnerving to observe hundreds of women cheering for their oppressors.

Personal property is allowed in limited amounts. Two boxes may be sent to you each year with clothes, shoes, craft and art supplies, and various other items. Once a week the commissary sells a selection of nonessential goods and a few necessities. There you can buy food, candy, yarn, Q-Tips and ·endless amounts of makeup, hair care products, and fingernail polish.

To qualify for Alderson you must be a low security risk, meaning that you have no record of violence or prison escape. You may arrive calm and nonviolent, but chances are you won't leave that way.

Alderson women live with a tremendous amount of frustration that belies the institution's outward appearance of serenity.

Like other prisons, it is filled with many who do not speak English. Their handicap is compounded by the fact that edicts which come trippingly off the tongues of the authorities sometimes are incomprehensible even when you know the language.

Example: On one occasion, the authorities called a "cottage" meeting (a euphemism for a dressing down of inmates for one reason or another). The particular crime this time was the unsightly condition of the rooms, especially the sight of waste paper in wastebaskets. Inmates were warned of dire consequences if the practice did not cease.

Not twenty-four hours later two Hispanic women appeared in tears at the unit manager's office. They had been caught with trash in their trash cans. Through an interpreter they explained that they had thought they must have misunderstood the orders. They promised not to use the wastebaskets again. After the interpreter relayed the story to the staff, the felons were asked to step outside into the hall. Five minutes later they were called back into the office and given ten hours of extra duty because ignorance of the law was no excuse. To insure that the offense would not occur again a written memo was posted in all of the cottages that trash found in the trash cans was a serious violation of prison rules. So inmates of all tongues walk around still wondering where to put their trash.

Strip searches are a common practice, especially for women in the hole. The practice has been curtailed for inmates receiving visitors—now it's left up to the discretion of the officer in charge. Some more than others like to look at naked women squatting and coughing. Censorship of incoming reading materials has now begun at Alderson. So far, the only book which has been rejected is one which is critical of the U.S. government.

Inmates generally get along well with each other. The greater problem lies in dealing with laziness and incompetence from above.

Visitors must be approved before coming through the gate. An arrest record and close association with other inmates are among the reasons for disapproval. Visiting days are Thursday, Friday, Saturday, Sunday, and Monday.

It is not a good idea to get sick while incarcerated. One Alderson woman complained of an eye irritation and was issued laxatives.

Mail is not read coming in or going out of this prison, but it is checked for contraband. You are not allowed to receive stamps through the mail. Checks are removed from incoming mail, endorsed in your name, and deposited to your account by the institution. Ironic that some women are incarcerated here for doing that same thing to other people's checks.

As prisons go Alderson is not the worst place to be. You will find it a test of your endurance of institutional stupidity meted out with a smile. But, as with all prisons, if you don't know how to steal, cheat, and lie you'll soon learn how. It's necessary for survival in this den of racketeers, profiteers, and thugs (otherwise known as prison officials).

11

Chicago

BUILT IN 1975 in downtown Chicago, the Metropolitan Correctional Center (MCC) is a twenty-six-story triangular skyscraper one block from the federal courthouse. Its long, slender, slotted windows make it look 'ike an IBM punch card. The gleaming plexiglass windows and the absence of bars, guntowers, and razor wire give this skyscraper prison the appearance of sterile respectability and the illusion of humaneness.

Like other MCCs in San Diego, New York, and Miami, this metropolitan lockup designed for both women and men primarily houses federal inmates who cannot make or are denied bond before trial and eventual sentencing. These prisoners are mainly young, poorly educated Blacks and Hispanics facing sentences of ten years and up for drug-related crimes. Next in number come the "holdovers," inmates awaiting transfer to other institutions. The third category, about one-fourth of the inmate population, are "cadre," the labor force that operates the institution. "Cadre" inmates are generally short-timers serving one year or less for nonviolent crimes.

MCC is a tough place, but violence between inmates is rare.

But make no mistake about it, MCC is hard time—damn hard time. Some say it's about the hardest time you can do.

For one thing, it is overcrowded. Being a sky-scraper, MCC has no yard for exercise and no place to escape tension, noise, and cigarette smoke. Except for a lucky few men assigned to work in the powerhouse, inmates at MCC never leave the building until released or transferred. The only access to open space, sunlight, and fresh air is a tiny, rooftop recreation cage available only twice a week during warm weather. With 600 prisoners warehoused in a space designed for 350, single cells doubled up, and with dormitory bunk beds only four to five feet apart, the building is a pressure cooker.

Compounding the overcrowding problem is the absence of recreational, social, and educational programs. For male prisoners there are no hobby or craft shops. The grimy, stuffy basement recreation area contains a basketball court, pool tables, and some exercise gear. Except for a G.E.D. course and a Spanish class, there are no educational programs. The library has a meager book collection and receives few newspapers and magazines. But inmates may receive books from the outside as well as magazine and newspaper subscriptions. The primary form of recreation is television watching. Each male living unit has at least four TV sets (but no cable access). Video cassette movies are shown on the weekends.

The twelfth floor houses all the female inmates—about forty-five. The unit is laid out in a triangle with the bedrooms lined up along the perimeter. The open center forms the dayroom and eating area. In one half of the triangle, consisting of two bedrooms complete with sink, toilet, shelves, desk, and lockers, women are locked in for head counts and bedtime. The other half of the floor consists of three dorm rooms with two or three double bunks in each room and two rooms with two beds each. These crowded rooms have small lockers for each resident. Three showers, four phones (collect calls only, 8 a.m. to 10 p.m., unlimited number of calls), two TVs, and a pool table complete the landscape.

A prison guard (male or female) is on duty at all times in the women's unit. The guard's attitude sets the tone. Some behave like housemothers; others are consumed by suspicion. They monitor and pat down the inmates, distribute mail, and inspect the bedrooms, picking through personal belongings in search of contraband. Rarely do the guards intervene in verbal disputes unless physical violence seems imminent.

Activities for women are rare to nonexistent except for meals, TV, and weekend video rentals (the slasher, basher, mass slaughter genre). A small conference room utilized for attorney visits doubles as an exercise room with its semi-functional stationary bike. Recreation is available about eight hours per week on the roof with a single basketball or in the dark basement with antiquated, unadjustable weight equipment. In the summer the roof is a popular place for sunbathing in improvised bikinis. Volunteers enlisted by the chaplain's office visit the women on Sundays, bringing yarn and other craft supplies. A steady stream of crocheted house slippers and baby sweaters departs weekly via the postal system.

Few female inmates have jobs at MCC. Laundry is the only off-floor job open to women. A few others are paid to do the heavy maintenance work on the unit and to microwave and serve the meals. The rest are responsible for keeping the rooms clean and the unit spiffy for the "show and fib" tours.

At MCC, the women inmates are a few fish in a sea of men, contributing to their isolation and dehumanization. There are mandatory Pap smears, tampons are not allowed, and clothes do not fit the female form. A meat market atmosphere reigns when women make trips off the floor. Strip searches are required after every contact visit.

Few women are assigned to serve sentences here, but sometimes they are held here for months or even years. A ready crew of inmate veterans provides support to newcomers. Your best asset here, as in other women's prisons, will be your fellow inmates.

Male inmates spend most if not all of the day in their units, each holding seventy to 120 residents and occupying two adjacent floors. Most live in two-man cells containing bunk beds, a writing desk, washbowl and toilet, and a long rectangular window. Meals are hauled up from the basement kitchen in refrigerated carts, heated in a microwave oven, and eaten at dining tables.

With four or eight telephones available to each unit, access is generally not a problem. Most floors also have an ice machine, a soda machine, a stationary exercise bicycle, and shower stalls.

Inmates are locked into their living quarters at 10 on weeknights, but if your unit passes the weekly inspection "late night" television viewing is permitted until midnight. The phones are cut off at 10 p.m. and turned on at 7:45 a.m. Recreation is available for two hours five times a week, including twice on the rooftop. There's nothing to do up there, but the sunlight and fresh air are healing.

The guards are constantly prowling around the rooms looking for food and eating utensils to confiscate, but harassment of inmates by staff is fairly minimal.

The most that can be said for the food is that extra milk, cereal, and fruit are usually available at breakfast and that on Fridays the cadre unit is treated to a non-microwaved buffet which includes raw vegetables.

Chicago is an excellent radio market, so a portable AM/FM radio is a wise investment. They cost $20 at the commissary, but used radios can often be purchased for $5 to $6 from inmates leaving the institution. (It is wise to sand off the inmate number of the old owner and get someone in one of the shops to engrave your number on the radio. Otherwise, the set may be confiscated.)

Cadre members are permitted visits twice weekly, four hours each time, in an eighth floor dining room. Body contact is allowed. Strip searches of the inmate follow all visits. (Rectal/vaginal finger probes do not occur unless you are suspected of possessing drugs. So don't worry when you see the guards put on the rubber gloves. They're just worried about germs.)

Movement within the building is only by elevator. A pass system is strictly enforced. Only two elevators serve the "secure" portion of the prison, one of which is reserved for the staff. It is, therefore, not uncommon to wait twenty minutes for a lift—a boon if you're headed to work, but an infuriating frustration if you are trying to reach the eighth floor for a visit.

What about work? Unless you're a carpenter or an electrician—and if you're male—you'll probably be assigned to wash dishes. This isn't as bad as it may sound. You'll have access to plenty of good food. But you'll also work overtime without pay. The dishroom schedule also cuts into your recreation time. Cook jobs pay well. With luck, you may eventually be assigned to the powerhouse—a boring job that gives you fresh air and time to read and write letters. Among the best jobs are librarian, chaplain's clerk, and lobby orderly. Do not expect any voice in your initial job assignment. After a short time of satisfactory performance, it is often possible to arrange a transfer, generally when the person holding the desired job is released or transferred. Most of the jobs pay the federal prison minimum of eleven cents an hour.

For a brief time MCC is tolerable. But many inmates spend two or three years here. That can be brutal. Some of the staff are cruel and manipulative. Others can be compassionate.

The hardest part about life in MCC is the initial shock. But after an adjustment period you may discover hidden reserves of strength, patience, and tolerance. You may also realize that you are more adaptable than you ever dreamt.

12

Fort Worth

THE YELLOW BRICK, red-roofed buildings of Fort Worth Federal Correctional Institution rise from a hill in the suburbs between Fort Worth and Dallas, Texas. Set back from the community on acres of well-manicured, inmate-tended lawn, behind a double chain-link fence topped by barbed wire, the institution commands a view of the Fort Worth skyline to the west. A former Veterans Administration hospital, the prison has a medical unit with wheelchair accessibility and a separate dining hall serving line for inmates having dietary restrictions.

Fort Worth FCI is also one of the few federal prisons with a "co-ed" population.* It has a combined "count" of around 1,000, with men generally outnumbering women.

The various floors of the building are designated as "living units," segregated by sex and drug-use history. Newcomers are assigned a bunk and locker in a dorm room housing ten to twenty. Lights and radios are supposed to be off after 10 p.m., but the rule is erratically enforced. No-smoking dorms are sometimes available.

* This account by a former woman inmate describes Fort Worth before the institution reverted to all-male status in October of 1988.

Inmates with seniority sleep in rooms for four, three, and two. When possible, you are given a choice of roommates.

The doors to the living units are open to the compound, but movement on the compound is restricted except for a few evening hours, and there is no access to other living units. Bathrooms, telephones, washers and dryers, and TV rooms are only barely adequate on each unit.

Mealtime in the high-ceilinged dining halls provides one of the few opportunities to see friends from other units; men and women wait in lines and sit at tables together. A dress code is enforced, and no reading materials may be brought in.

Men and women may mingle on the compound, a square of untouchable grass with concrete walkways and some benches, but a "no physical contact" rule is strictly enforced. This creates an atmosphere in which one would think twice before even reaching out to touch a friend's hand in comfort. With more inmates than benches, couples will often walk around and around the compound, talking. A man and a woman who are seen together regularly are thus called "walkies." Predictably, talking or walking with "someone else's" walkie takes on a significance unequaled since early high school.

In this bizarre atmosphere, pornography abounds, and competition for and between women is intense; much emphasis is put on appearance. The "no physical contact" rule is often violated, sometimes with the help of such ingenious trappings as pants with holes cut in the crotch.

The recreation yard or job assignment site most often provides the settings for such sexual encounters, and, try as one might, it is difficult to remain ignorant of another's affairs (so to speak).

The recreation yard meets the description of a resort: tennis and racquetball courts, a track, weight shack, a miniature golf course. But the absence of trees, the nearby fences, and the watchful eyes of guards quickly dispel that illusion. Only a few hours are available for coed recreation.

Work assignments are housekeeping jobs on the living unit or elsewhere in the institution. The prison industry system operates computer processing and printing shops in Fort Worth. Generally, this work will take six or seven hours a day.

Visitors to the institution will notice an attempt to create "normal" surroundings, with woven hangings on the walls inside, and some limited playground equipment in an outdoor visiting yard. The dress code for visitors forbids shorts, bare midriff areas, and halter tops. Women visitors must wear bras.

13

Sandstone

THE SANDSTONE Federal Correctional Institution, about ninety miles north of Minneapolis, houses some 850 prisoners from throughout the United States, and from other countries, mostly Hispanics for whom English is a second language. The prison consists of a central core of continuously connected buildings facing an inner compound park with lawn, trees, walks, and benches. To the east is a large outdoor recreational area connected to the inner compound by a passageway. To the south are shops, administrative office buildings, and factories which form three sides of a square.

A phone call to the prison will be useful in determining what you may or may not bring. If you are entering the system for the first time you will be discouraged from bringing anything. Insist on being told what nonclothing items you may bring. The rules permit one musical instrument, books, Walkman-type (non-cassette) radio, athletic shoes and clothing, and toilet articles. You will be issued prison clothing, towel, bed linen, toilet articles, and laundry soap. The prison also furnishes free envelopes, writing paper, and greeting cards. If possible bring a $50 postal money order with you so that you may open a commissary account.

Initially you will be housed with about eighty prisoners in a large room subdivided into cubes by shoulder-high partitions. You will be assigned a bunk and locker and will share the shelf space and writing desk with your cubemate. Each housing unit has two TV rooms, with tables for card and game playing. The units have common toilet rooms, lavatory rooms, showers, a washer and dryer, an ice machine and water fountain, and steaming water dispenser. They also have offices for the unit guard and for prison staff members who make up your "team."

Meals are served cafeteria style in two lines. Soup and a salad bar are available at lunch and dinner. Those who have experienced institutional cooking will find the food average to above average and it is not difficult to enjoy a balanced diet. You will gain weight if you eat all meals served and do not exercise. The prison bakery turns out a variety of rolls and sweets designed to fatten you up.

Gym and recreational facilities are extensive.

Federal prisoners are required to work. Refusal to do so will result in solitary confinement. In theory, each prisoner may eventually select the type of work he wishes. Federal Prison Industries, operating as UNICOR, manufactures a variety of gloves and operates a printing plant at Sandstone. Wage rates are the highest paid in the prison, 11 cents to $1.40 per hour. At these slave labor rates it competes with outside business to supply products to a variety of government agencies, the military, and military contractors. To work at UNICOR you must agree to pay fines and restitution under the Financial Responsibility Program with a prearranged portion of the earnings.

Other jobs fall into two broad categories—those that assist the well-being of your fellow prisoners (cooking, cleaning, chapel orderly, etc.), and those that serve the interest of the prison administration and its employees, such as outside construction jobs, administration office and clerical jobs, and outside maintenance jobs.

Some other things for the Sandstone newcomer to keep in mind:

As at other penal institutions, there is a drug testing program at Sandstone. You will be asked to pee in a bottle while a guard watches to be sure that what's in the bottle you hand back to him contains the real thing and that it's yours. Refusal to cooperate is treated as seriously as assaulting a guard or running weapons, punishable by banishment to the hole, loss of "good time," and transfer to another prison. Hope that the folks who process and analyze your sample do it properly. If not, the consequences of a bad urine are the same as refusing to pee.

Beware of the financial responsibility program, designed by Caesar to make prisoners pay restitution, fees, back-taxes, fines, and other debts. It is voluntary. Refusal to become financially responsible will limit your prison earnings to $5 per month, the equivalent of 3 cents an hour.

You will be asked to attend quarterly "team" meetings with your unit manager (usually male), case manager, or correctional counselor (always female) to review your progress in becoming robotized. You will be asked, how are you?, how's your work?, are you having any problems? Recommended replies are fine, fine, and no, in that order. Anything else by way of response will cause squirming, frowns, clearing of throats, and little if any remedial action. These meetings may be skipped.

"The Hole" is one of the ultimate threats used in behavior modification at Sandstone and most other federal prisons—along with loss of good time and transfer to another institution. Being sent to the hole is what you decide to make it. You will usually have a private cell; you will eat the same meals as other inmates, but the food will be delivered to your door. You will be allowed out of the cell for one hour on weekdays for recreation and three times a week for a shower and change of clothes. Eventually you will get some of your books and writing materials. Usually the surroundings will be quiet, conducive to reading and writing, prayer, meditation, and reflection. All in all, not a bad way to get away from the daily routine. A three to seven-day fast is recommended to start your stay in the hole. Not only will this help you focus your thoughts and energy and offset weight gain from the inactivity, it will also create the impression that you are staging a hunger strike. That will drive the guards right up the wall.

For prisoners of conscience, the time spent in prison can be a rich and rewarding experience. There are daily opportunities to continue the witness which brought you here in the first place. Living each day alert to ways to assist your fellow prisoners, to continue your work for peace and justice, and to resist the evil represented by jails and prisons will make your time pass quickly. It will be good time.

An ancient Latin expression seems appropriate for prisoners and for resisters, "Nihil Illegitimati Corborundum"—or, "Don't Let the Bastards Wear You Down." The Spirit which moved you to do what brought you to Sandstone will sustain you while you are here.

14

Terre Haute Camp

THE TERRE HAUTE Federal Prison Camp is in southwestern Indiana, a four-hour drive south of Chicago and one and a half hours west of Indianapolis. It is a satellite of the nearby Terre Haute Penitentiary for more serious offenders. The countryside is green and fertile farmland, much too nice to be polluted by a prison.

Terre Haute FPC is one of the oldest of the federal prison camps. Built for 200, it now holds twice that number.

The camp is also a Bureau of Prisons bus center, a place where federal prisoners spend a few days on their way to other institutions. Prison buses arrive or depart a couple of times a week. You can recognize the "holdover" inmates by the prison issue blue slippers they are required to wear.

The camp uniform consists of Army greens with black work shoes. Prisoners are allowed personal leisure clothes if they buy them at the commissary or brought them from another federal institution, or have them sent in from the outside.

Most of the prisoners are from Illinois, Indiana, Kentucky, Michigan, Ohio, and Tennessee. Many are from Chicago and Detroit. Despite occasional tension, there are few fights.

There is a mood of anger and bitterness toward the federal government. As at other prison camps, most of the prisoners seem to have been committed for drug-related offenses. There are also a good many "white collar criminals" and the occasional tax-protester and peace activist.

The camp's main building is a red brick structure that looks like one of the high schools built all over the country in the 1950s. It houses the camp's eight dorms, main desk, offices, cafeteria, commissary, visiting room, gym, and recreation rooms. Other buildings house the school, chapel, factory, farm, and various support services. The recreation yard has a running track, ball field, tennis courts, miniature golf course, horse-shoe pit, and handball court.

There are no fences, but the boundaries are clearly understood. There is not much room to roam, and the staff keeps a close eye on those who do.

People work hard at having fun here. They work at softball, backgammon, gin, spades, ping-pong, pool, chess, cribbage, tennis, miniature golf, racquetball, handball, and dominoes.

Softball is especially big—and competitive, with crowds coming to the games. A varsity softball team plays teams from the outside. All of its games, as you would expect, are home games.

Terre Haute is a work camp. All inmates are expected to have jobs. You can work in food service, as a janitorial orderly, on the landscape crew, on the farm, or in the prison factory. Some jobs are full time, others are part time.

Most of the jobs start at 11 cents an hour with occasional increases. The highest paying jobs are in the UNICOR factory, which produces towels and washcloths for government agencies, including the Pentagon.

UNICOR jobs are sought after by prisoners with heavy fines to pay or families to support. But working conditions are stressful.

A few prefer to work on the prison farm, where vegetables are grown on thirty-five acres of cultivated land. It's hard labor in the hot sun for long hours, but the job offers plenty of fresh air, the sense of doing something useful, and the fun of digging in the dirt.

Work at the camp gives prisoners something to do and a few bucks a week for the commissary. But it's also a form of slave labor. Some prisoners resent the required work. They feel they were sentenced to do their time, but not time with hard labor, which went out with the whip and the stocks.

The food is simple and starchy, but edible. Many supplement the dining room fare with food from the commissary and vending machines.

The prison camp has eight dormitories, each holding about fifty-five men. Rooms hold from two to sixteen residents in double-decker bunks. The bathrooms are crowded during rush hours and offer little privacy. Sitting on the toilet is an exercise in egalitarianism.

The chapel is a good place to escape the crowds. The Protestant theology here is Southern Evangelical, with an emphasis on being saved. A Catholic priest comes in for Mass on Tuesday nights. The Sisters of Divine Providence attend some services and bring a kindly influence with them. The camp also receives service from a Muslim chaplain, who spends most of his time at the main prison.

Health care at the camp leaves much to be desired. Inmates are seen by physicians' assistants, who are pressed for time. Physicians from the main prison drop by the camp occasionally. The care may be good when you can get it, but there are tales of long delays in receiving necessary attention to medical problems.

The camp offers a small legal library, a small reading library, and classrooms at the Education Center. The pride of the Center is the Diesel Mechanic Training School, run by Vincennes University. Student maintenance mechanics practice on the prison buses which come through.

Prisoners who violate the rules are sent to "the hole," or segregation. They are locked in two-man cells twenty-three hours a day. The staff sends about one man a week to the hole, usually for a short period of time. Sometimes the offenses seem trivial—like failing to stay in place until the count is cleared.

Each inmate is assigned a counselor and a case manager. These people are overworked and it usually takes a long time to get business taken care of and paperwork processed. Prisoners can be inconvenienced and hurt by these delays because nothing can be accomplished before the paperwork is completed. Because of such delays, for example, it can sometimes take months for friends and loved ones to receive the necessary permission to visit.

The outdoors, recreation activities, and the chapel help prisoners cope. Living at Terre Haute Camp is like living at a strict boarding school. (There are far worse places depicted in the novels of Charles Dickens.)

Terre Haute Camp is no country club. But there are worse places to spend your prison time. It offers an opportunity to learn about prisons, about the world, about people, and about yourself.

15

Oxford Camp

YOUR IMPRESSION of Oxford Federal Prison Camp will depend, at least initially, on where you've been previously. Because it's a facility for low-risk, nonviolent inmates (level 1), many arrivals "self-surrender"; for most of these, this will be their first incarceration. Such elements as lack of privacy, tight quarters, common menu (rather high in cholesterol content), meaningless rules and restrictions, and separation from family, friends, and familiar surroundings will prove traumatic. For those who come from other penal institutions, Oxford may seem a paradise. And for those "on the other side of fifty," it can be a comfortable nursing home—a bungalow with four protruding dormitory wings, built for 104 with capacity for 160, laid out in a remote woodsy area of Wisconsin's mid-section.

Oxford Camp was built in 1985, some surmise as a protective resort for "snitches," those who "rat" on other defendants or inmates. In reality, it's a "satellite camp" for the high level (4 and 5) prison located a couple of football fields away on the same federal grounds. Compared with other prison camps (most of them considerably larger, the walking and playing space at Oxford is sparse. Beside the roadway circling the building there is a tennis court and ballfield, around which one can walk or run. Tiny red signs dot the perimeter with "out of bounds" warnings. A three-foot wall encloses a patio at the front of the building where, in good weather, you can entertain visitors on approved days.

In addition to your immediate family (parents, wife, children, siblings, in-laws, nieces, nephews, grandchildren), you will be allowed ten others on a separate visiting list, all of whom have to be approved before visiting begins—and some of whom may take months to approve. The visiting room is small, with the overflow limited to the library, and occasionally the chapel. Visits are limited to Saturdays and Sundays.

There is plenty of food, some of it of the poorest quality. As almost everywhere else in the prison system, meals are too early—breakfast at 6:30 a.m., lunch at 10:30, and dinner at 3:30 or 4 in the afternoon. No matter how long the line, the entire meal for everyone has to be over within half an hour. You may have to gulp down a meal in less than ten minutes in order to be on time for "count." (At several specified times throughout the day and night you have to be in your room, usually, to be counted. On one occasion a new inmate woke up in the middle of the night to take a pee; since he was in the bathroom during "count" he was punished with four and a half hours of "extra time" work.)

Thirty to forty inmates occupied each of the four wings and each room had three or four inmates until mid-1989, when a new policy began reducing the inmate population from 140 to 112. Compared with county jails and other prisons, Oxford does not seem crowded. However, there is considerable congestion in the showers and bathrooms. Often only eight showers are available and the trick is to find one with hot or warm water. Another problem is the noise. Acoustically, the entire place is a disaster—but especially

the visiting room and TV rooms. Sounds coming out of the TV can be unintelligible.

About half the inmates at Oxford Camp are in for drug-related crimes. There's a preponderance of professionals, including judges, lawyers, doctors, pharmacists, pilots, businessmen. A basic mutual respect and courtesy seems to prevail, despite aggravations caused by living in tight quarters. There is also a variety of ethnic and national backgrounds. Most of the guards are respectful, caring individuals.

In mid-1989 the only doctor in attendance quit, leaving physicians' assistants to minister to medical needs. Outside of medical and dental emergencies you should be prepared for a great deal of waiting and for minimal care.

Cleanliness is sometimes made into a fetish, especially in the waxing and buffing of floors. On the other hand, bathrooms and recreational areas become pigsties on weekends.

Mail is distributed from 5 to 5:30 p.m. in the visiting room or patio. As in other prisons, incoming mail is opened, checked for contraband, and sometimes read.

Four phones are available. But be prepared to wait, especially during evening hours.

Several "orderly" (i.e., cleaning) jobs are available, as well as work in maintenance crews, power-house, and kitchen. These jobs pay $5 per month. Until the program was phased out in June 1989, jobs paying up to $100 a month were available at UNICOR, a privately run prison industry which, at Oxford, built military cables for the Pentagon.

Protestant and Catholic religious services are available once a week, Jewish services about once or twice a month, and also Ramadan services at appropriate times. None of the chaplains spends much time at the camp, barely the forty-five minutes a week or so required for the weekly services. Their main focus is at the large prison.

Oxford has a small gym with one basketball net, body-building equipment, ping-pong, pool, card-playing, TV, VCR movies on weekends. Outdoor activities include jogging, walks, tennis, horse-shoes, baseball.

Oxford Camp has been characterized as a "country club." Inmates find this generalization misleading. The place lacks barbed-wire, walls, and guards with guns, but freedom is curtailed, and the heartaches connected with incarceration are as acute as at other facilities.

16

Marion Camp

MARION FEDERAL PRISON CAMP at Marion, Illinois, is a satellite of the nation's highest level maximum security prison, the notorious Marion Penitentiary, where inmates have been locked in their cells since 1983. The function and tenor of the camp are shaped by the grim reality of life behind the walls.

With the penitentiary's 450 inmates "locked down" for all but an hour each day, it is up to the camp's 225 residents to do the prison's daily "housekeeping" tasks, work in the carpentry, electrical, and plumbing shops, and carry out other functions normally assigned to prisoners.

An incoming prisoner's first impressions are formed inside the main prison, where he reports for initial processing. If he arrives on a Friday, during a weekend, or before a holiday, he'll spend his first nights behind the wall in a dormitory which also serves as "the hole" for the camp.

Once processed into camp, you are likely to be assigned for the first three months or so to the prison kitchen. There is no self-supporting kitchen in the camp. Food for all prisoners comes from behind the walls.

A few jobs are to be found in the camp itself, but most prisoners work behind the walls in the administration area, in mechanical services, and in the expanding prison factory, which produces military cables.

Working in the bowels of this fortress from 7:30 in the morning to 3:30 in the afternoon, you'll catch glimpses of these "high risk" prisoners and the conditions to which they are subjected. It's a depressing experience.

In 1989 a new camp dormitory was constructed to replace an older dormitory and two trailers which offered privileged housing. The new dormitory is of concrete block, with unmovable bottleglass windows, central heating, and air conditioning. The older buildings are of corrugated steel.

One of the original dormitories remained open for housing, allowing fifty-five inmates with seniority to live in single occupancy cubicles furnished with bunk, chair, a desk, locker, and shelves. In the new building the cubicles are designed for two to four occupants.

Educational programs and facilities are limited at Marion Camp. A G.E.D. program is offered by the staff; inmates offer occasional classes in such subjects as Spanish and business. The camp has an abbreviated law library and a sundry collection of discarded books for general reading.

Recreational facilities consist of a cinder track, baseball diamond, hand/racquetball court, tennis court, and a gymnasium offering half-court basketball and weight-lifting paraphernalia.

Half of this gymnasium has been requisitioned for a new visiting area. Visiting out of doors is allowed in a restricted area when weather permits. It is possible to have as many as ten approved visitors, with up to five adults allowed to visit simultaneously. Twenty visits per month are allowed; visiting hours are from 8 a.m. to 3 p.m. on Friday, Saturday, Sunday, Monday, and federal holidays. As at other prison camps, inmates and visitors are allowed physical contact.

No real medical facilities exist in the camp. Physicians' assistants come each morning for "routine treatment." More serious problems are referred to a staff doctor in the main prison. The most serious cases are transferred to federal prison hospitals at Springfield, Missouri, or Rochester, Minnesota, or, on rare occasions, treated locally.

If you are a vegetarian you had better be a good forager. The food service department does not assign a diet tray for the non-meat eater.

The camp compound is on an edge of the Shawnee National Forest preserve, well away from the sights and sounds of the town of Marion and nearby Carbondale, site of Southern Illinois University. But on some nights you can hear the distant hum of the highway and see the glow of city lights in the sky. These blend with the roar of sulphurous coal smoke belching from the prison powerhouse and the glare of arc lights on the prison walls.

And then there is the matter of the institution's water supply. Crab Orchard Lake, where the water comes from, is so toxic that nearby towns have found alternative sources and the federal Environmental Protection Agency has put it on the superfund cleanup list. The lake is rich in lead, PCB's, and other poisons. The Bureau of Prisons says it is satisfied that the water supply is clean enough. Despite several lawsuits, it refuses to make further tests.

17

Yankton Camp

THE MISSION of Yankton Federal Prison Camp in Yankton, South Dakota, is the building of additional facilities for the U.S. Bureau of Prisons. "We are essentially a work camp," Superintendent Stephen F. Pontesso tells new arrivals.

For inmates willing to lend themselves to that purpose, Yankton offers as pleasant an environment as you'll find in the federal prison system.

The camp was established in mid-1988 on the campus of Yankton College, a liberal arts school which opened in 1881 as the first institution of higher learning in South Dakota, reached an enrollment peak in the 1960s, declined in the 1970s, and was closed by its creditors in 1984.

Purchased by the federal government as part of a national prison expansion program, Yankton reached an inmate population of about 200 by mid-1989, the number swelling with the refitting and renovation of each college building. The population target is 500.

Newcomers to the prison camp are carefully screened to meet the needs of the institution and the community which surrounds it. The inmates are better educated and more mature than most prisoners. All are deemed minimum security risks—needing no physical confinement. Most are white, middle-class males convicted of white collar crimes.

Unguarded by fences or watchtowers, the camp is in a tidy residential neighborhood of a city of 12,000,

across the street from homes where the quiet is disturbed only by the occasional shrieks of children at play and the roar of a lawnmower. A few inconspicuous signs identify the facility as a penal institution. The prisoners themselves, dressed in crisp khaki uniforms and sturdy black boots, could easily be mistaken for ROTC students on their way to class.

The camp offers a library, gymnasium, tennis courts, running track, and television/recreation rooms for smokers and nonsmokers. Inmates live four to a room in a modern, handsomely appointed dormitory where the doors are never locked. Aside from the need to report for work, show up for head counts, and remain within the camp boundaries, there are few restrictions on inmates' movements.

Yankton's dormitory has six public telephones from which collect calls can be made from midafternoon until past midnight on weekdays and at any time on weekends. Inmates can receive visitors on Thursday and Friday evenings and on Saturdays and Sundays in indoor and outdoor visiting areas.

Work hours are from 7:30 a.m. to 3:30 p.m., with an hour off for lunch. There are the traditional prison jobs in food service, mopping, sweeping, clerking, and groundskeeping, but the main emphasis at Yankton is on preparing the college's physical plant for prison use. Work crews rip up old sidewalks and pour concrete for new ones, repair and renovate old buildings, fix roofs, paint woodwork, convert science laboratories into offices and inmate living space.

UNICOR, the quasi-public manufacturing company that employs federal prisoners at wages up to $1.40 an hour, has no outlet at Yankton. So the top pay is 11 cents an hour, or $5 a month for newcomers. Despite this, morale is high, even among inmates with construction skills commanding $20 an hour on the outside. It is not uncommon for some to volunteer for extra duty on weekends.

Partly this is because hard and useful work makes the time go faster. But the high morale is also attributable to a gung-ho spirit carefully inculcated by the staff. For the most part, officers treat inmates with courtesy, respect, and an easy informality. Disciplinary cases are few and far between. The mood at Yankton is definitely up-beat.

On one Saturday in May the prison staff treated inmates to an "inmate appreciation day," consisting of a softball game, a tug-of-war tournament, horseshoe pitching, and T-bone steaks topped off with ice cream and strawberry shortcake.

Some inmates complained that the steaks were a little tough. Indeed, the food and quality of service at the Yankton mess hall set a high standard. Inmates and staff members sit in groups of four at tables laid with fresh cloths and decorated with flowers. The food is varied, tasty, and plentiful, including salad bar at the noon and evening meals. The eating at Yankton is as good as you'll find at most commercial restaurants.

Sacred Heart, a Benedictine convent, only a twenty-minute walk from the camp, will provide hospitality for visitors of imprisoned peace activists. Contact the prioress for details.

If you happen to be a male federal prisoner and you don't mind helping the government build room for more, then Yankton prison camp is the place to be.

18

Leavenworth Camp

A quarter-mile west of the looming movie-set guard towers of Leavenworth Federal Penitentiary, across a field where bison graze, is a red brick structure that looks from the outside like a small college dorm. From the inside, it more resembles an army barracks: the minimum security federal prison camp at Leavenworth, Kansas, or LVC as postal authorities dubbed it.

The prison is built to house 280 prisoners; like most U.S. prisons, the population seldom gets that low. Six of the eight dormitory wings house barracks; if you are a relative long-termer who behaves, you might be fortunate enough to share a dorm room with one other person. The food is generally good for being institutional—better than college cafeteria food, at any rate.

Common offenses that bring people to the camp are fraud, drugs, and immigrating. More exotic crimes have included bilking General Motors out of $40 million in a phony rent-a-car scheme, and contempt of Congress for refusing to testify about the Kansas City mob.

All prisoners are expected to work. Wages run from 11 cents an hour for work in the kitchen or as an orderly, to $1.40 for work with UNICOR (federal prison industries). Industries associated with the camp are the mattress factory and the mattress tick factory, the former being relatively hard work in dusty conditions, the latter being pretty easy, and in clean conditions.

Leavenworth County probably has the highest concentration of prisoners of any county in the country. The area's dependence on prisons stems not only from LVC and the federal maximum security prison, but also from the military prison at Fort Leavenworth and the men's and women's state prisons in nearby Lansing.

IV

Prisoners On Purpose

19
Personal Stories

A House of Mirrors

PRISON HAS BEEN a journey into the deep desert of my own soul. Loneliness, isolation from loved ones, absence of physical touch, and separation from nature have broken me open like a seed sprouting in the earth's womb. Stripped of the illusions imposed by my bourgeois education, and immersed in an alien, hostile world, I was flung into a collision with myself. Having learned to construct my identity on what I *did*, I found myself unprepared for the task of simply *being*. What does it mean simply to be in our goal-oriented, outer-directed culture?

Prison proved to be an inescapable house of mirrors reflecting my inner self. Instead of noble dimensions of my being, what I saw was frequently ugly, violent, selfish, and hateful. Far from being the contented, contemplative, Gandhi-like peace activist I had pictured to myself, I discovered a raging Vesuvius of bitterness, frustration, and animosity. Having been raised in an upper-middle class family, and having become used to the privileged position of a well-educated white male in a patriarchal society, I was stunned to find myself suddenly powerless and a pariah.

The noise, cigarette smoke, and jam-packed humanity overwhelmed me. Cut off from friends and loved ones, I felt terribly alone and vulnerable, as if I were underwater breathing through a straw, living on the edge of panic and suffocation. Gradually, however, I discovered that the things that most aggravated me about others' behavior were the very same traits I was most ashamed of in myself—selfishness, insensitivity, pettiness, intolerance. My antipathy toward others was in fact a projection of my own inner brokenness.

As a matter of simple psychological survival, I was forced to confront the reality of who I am. Somehow in the darkness my eyes began to see. In learning self-awareness I became more receptive to the Great Spirit and began to appreciate prison as a great gift, a fertile field for spiritual exploration. Now I understand that to be filled with wisdom one must first through suffering be emptied of the illusions and false dependencies.

To simply *be* instead of being obsessed with *doing* continues to be my toughest test. For I am still too often impatient and demanding. Yet through my willing surrender into suffering, uncertainty, and spiritual/emotional nakedness, the fire of this experience is annealing and healing me.

One needn't be a hero in prison; being fully human is enough. We may feel lonely, but it is impossible to be alone because a great web of compassion unites resisters all over the planet. With the grace of God, the love of my friends, and the strength of fellow inmates, I have survived my immersion in the dragon's belly—and thus am liberated from my fear.

I cry a lot more these days; everything seems to affect me deeply. I think that's because my heart has grown softer. Prison has taught me that I am much more (and much less) than I ever imagined. Prison has helped me become more of what I want to be—one who can fully love others.—**Duane Bean**

A Fugitive from 'Justice'

IN MARCH OF 1989 I received a letter from the pre-trial services office of the U.S. District Court in Kansas City requesting that I please call to make arrangements to be indicted for two missile launch site entries, and politely thanking me for my cooperation. I felt a certain reluctance to "cooperate" with these polite people, whose ultimate goal was to put me in the slammer for a year. Besides, my husband and I had vacation plans.

Repressing a twinge of guilt for failing to politely respond, we took off for a month in the West. Upon our return, I found myself the victim of a growing paranoia. "If the phone rings, I'm outta town"; "If someone's at the door, I'm not home"; "Who's that stranger out front?"

Whoa. Wait a minute, I thought. Noncooperation is one thing, but this fugitive business isn't all that much fun.

A visit with friend Jean Gump at the federal prison in Alderson, West Virginia, did wonders for my sanity. I returned to Chicago and my activism, and managed to get arrested doing some guerrilla theater on El Salvador's election day. Two of us "died" at the hands of a death squad and ended up floating limply in the fountain at Daley Plaza, a deed for which we were charged with "wading in a public fountain without a permit."

I came home from a demo on June 1st to learn the FBI in Kansas City had called, politely asking that I return the call. Later, I thought. I had plans to visit friends in Wisconsin. The following Wednesday, my husband called to tell me three FBI agents had arrived at our home at 6:30 that morning politely asking for Elizabeth Lewis.

After being allowed to search the house, one of the agents asked Jim, "Why is she doing this? We should be out catching real criminals." It seemed time to head for Kansas City.

But first I had a court appearance for fountain wading. Friends cautioned me that the FBI might be waiting to apprehend me, but I felt that bureaucracy being what it is, there was small likelihood that one hand knew what the other was doing. The charges were dismissed and I was free to go.

On June 12th, I sat in the Federal Building courtroom in Kansas City while Katie Willems was on trial. Surely I would soon feel a polite tap on the shoulder, but none came. The next day I "cooperated" and turned myself in.—**Betty Lewis**

Don't Forget to Leave
the Comb

YOU'RE FROM ALDERSON?

Know Jean Gump?

Where you headed for?

The sharing of information, destinations, a precious comb, were the tenuous ties that bound me to other inmates at the women's transportation center in Norman, Oklahoma, officially known as the Cleveland County Detention Center (CCDC).

To withstand the oppression we had humor, hands that braid hair, ears that listen.

It's hard to forget the sights and sounds:

The intercom blasts a woman's last name in the wee hours of the morning. "Get all your stuff together and go to the door." Roommates hug and wish each other luck. We press our faces against the windows of our cells to see which friends are leaving, to remind them to leave the comb behind, and to reassure ourselves that people do leave.

We learned to make do. We found out that gym shoes make erasers, that sanitary napkins can be converted to tampons, that toilet paper can serve as hair curlers. Some discovered they could get what they needed by being politely obnoxious, persistent, and calling the guards by name.

We found ourselves in a melting pot. Lifers met first timers and discussed Alderson vs. Lexington, co-ed vs. all-women prisons. Check forgers mixed with murderers and talked about their kids.

We discovered or rediscovered how to cope with zoo-like conditions. Some of us endured by staying in our rooms, sleeping, listening to the freight trains whistle and rock past the jail. Others sought male contact by passing notes, or perching on the sink to converse with men in "the hole." Some isolated themselves in front of the TV. A few made themselves vulnerable by reminding the guards of every prisoner's humanity and the reasonableness of their needs.

All of us felt a perverse joy at the sound of jingling chains, signaling the approach of the federal marshals, shackling time, and departure from the Cleveland County Detention Center.—**Katey Feit**

Free for a While

ONE EVENING at the D.C. Jail in Washington my automatic cell door popped open and I was told to pack my things.

Since I had served only one month of an eleven-month sentence I figured the marshals had come to take me to some federal prison. I sacked up my belongings and reported to the Receiving and Discharge office. But instead of the marshals I found my clerical attire awaiting me.

After dressing in my civilian clothes I was ushered into another room, asked my name and number, given a bus token, and told to take the second gate on the left. It led to the street. I asked no questions but kept moving to the third bus stop. As I arrived there a bus pulled in, I got on, sat down, and then started laughing.

What the heck was happening?

After about half an hour of seeing no recognizable landmark I pulled the cord and got off. I walked to a pay phone, got directions to a Catholic Worker house, and ultimately made my way to the home of friends in Baltimore.

Several weeks later, on the eve of my birthday, my mother called from our farm in Illinois to tell me that a federal marshal had come out to the house "looking for Carl." She also said my brother Paul had called from Minnesota to say that two federal marshals were on my trail there.

It seemed a "mistake" had been made in letting me out.

Since my release occurred just five days before Pope John Paul II was to visit Washington, my guess is that the mistake was a calculated one. At the time I was the only Catholic priest in the country in jail—and in the very city that the Pope was to visit.

Were the authorities worried that the Pope, while dining with the President, might inquire about the jailed priest?

A month later I turned myself in and served the rest of my sentence. —**Carl Kabat**

A Visit to a County Jail

HERE IS A STORY a Missouri Peace Planting supporter told me about her first visit to a county jail following a missile silo action in 1986: "I didn't know the two peace activists I was going to see, but I knew of them through mutual friends. I felt that this was one way I could begin to put into action the beliefs I had espoused for so long. I was completely unprepared for the experience.

"When I arrived, laden with sacks of food, books, sheets, and writing materials, I found visitors were not even allowed inside until the designated hour. The steps were lined with families waiting in the hot sun; some carried boxes of supplies and had young children in tow. Some had come from as far away as Iowa and Nebraska for this two-hour visit. As I stood among these people I began to feel very humble and very much aware of my middle-class security.

"Eventually an officer swung the door open and began letting people in by threes. Every purse, box, sack, and letter was searched, thus stealing precious minutes from the allowed two hours. The system seemed random and arbitrary. Food might be allowed in for one prisoner but not for another. When my turn came, the two officers balked at some ground coffee I had brought in a plastic container. I tried to walk the fine line between pleading with them and annoying them. Finally one guard smiled and said, 'You can take it in. I'm feeling generous today.' I had to bite my tongue; I knew I was up against absolute power.

"Next I was directed to go into an office and then through another door. The second door looked as though it opened into a closet, but the 'closet' turned out to be a short, narrow, dim passageway that smelled of urine. I found out later that I was in the holding tank, a primitive, dismal area where prisoners are supposedly held only a few days.

"The two peace activists had been there for weeks. I called their names, and from the back cell eager voices began yelling, 'Here we are! We're back here!' And suddenly I was looking into two friendly, smiling, perspiring faces peering at me through bars. I don't know if I successfully hid my dismay at their surroundings.

"Five men were in a cell the size of a large walk-in closet. There were two two-tiered bunks to the left and one to the right. There was a toilet in a cubicle the size of a small broom closet. Some of the bunks had sheets and some didn't. There was no privacy, no space, no ventilation, no natural light. The one window, on the visitors' side of the bars, was covered with sheet metal. The men ate, sat, and slept in their bunks. They were taken upstairs for exercise every ten days to two weeks.

"Despite their circumstances, the two men were jovial, optimistic, generous, and loving. Their concern for fellow inmates was touching. From their own supplies they shared cigarettes and snacks for men who had no one to visit them.

"A young boy had been placed in their cell for safety. He had been suffering abuse from some other prisoners so a guard had transferred him to the cell of the two peace activists, saying, 'You'll be safe here.' Their generosity and selflessness in these difficult surroundings strengthened my own commitment to doing something for the cause of peace." —**Janice Dover**

Grey Is the Color of the Sky

AFTER FIVE WEEKS in the Cass County Jail I was finally going to bond out. I had hoped to stay in through the trial and sentencing, but trial preparation was next to impossible from inside the jail. My ticket out was a letter from the magistrate saying that he would release me on my promise not to enter another missile launch site—a condition I had refused at my arraignment. I was ready to go, but anxious, because the guard at the jail seemed sure I would be back.

I stayed up most of the night playing Yahtzee and talking with the other women in the cell. I had a few belongings to give away, but the guard was so insistent that I wasn't being released. Should I pack my bags and be ready to go, anyway? I decided to wait. Maybe the judge had changed his mind. One of my co-conspirators had trespassed at a nuclear silo while he was out on bond, so perhaps there would be no more bonds for us. Could I really stand the food and the closed-in space that much longer? With these and other worries, I eventually fell asleep in the early morning hours.

Around 6 a.m., a guard brought my clothes to me and told me to get ready to go to court—but not to pack my belongings. Most of the women were still asleep, so I moved quietly, taking a shower, getting dressed in my "street clothes," talking softly to the other woman who was going with me. She was looking forward to being flown to Lexington Women's Prison. Traveling with the U.S. marshals is a miserable way to fly, but anything would be better than remaining here.

Quiet as we were, each of my cellmates awakened long enough to say goodbye before the marshals came. The metal door opened; we left the cell, were searched, handcuffed, chained at the waist and shackled at the legs, and, after much delay, taken outside for our ride to Kansas City.

It had been a long time since I had seen the sunlight for any length of time. I had to squint as we stood outside the van. When my turn came, I climbed clumsily into the back and slid into the seat next to my companion. We didn't say much. She was going back to prison after breaking a rule at a "halfway house"; I was, hopefully, on my way out.

The wait in the holding cell downtown seemed interminable. We were the only two women in the small room with two hard benches and a toilet for furniture. I had my legal papers with me but nothing suitable for light reading. We curled up on our benches and dozed fitfully.

The marshals came for me first. I was handcuffed once again and led downstairs with the other prisoners by way of the freight elevator, so the sight of us wouldn't embarrass the public, or the judges.

In the courtroom, I saw the familiar faces: supporters from Kansas City; people from my own community in Milwaukee; my two beloved co-conspirators, Dorothy and Jerry, and their attorney; the prosecuting attorney and other government employees. My handcuffs were removed. I took a second look around and saw the pretrial services representative there—a good sign? I didn't notice any paperwork with him; that was not a good sign.

Jerry and Dorothy and I embraced, waved to our friends in the pews, and spent a few minutes trying to catch up on each other's news. We stumbled through our "pretrial conference" with the help of the lawyer, and the magistrate made a passing reference to my scheduled release on bond. A very good sign!

I had to listen to him read through all fourteen standard conditions of the bond, plus some extra ones, although I'd heard them all before. His voice droned on and on. At last, he was ready for signatures. I scrawled my name on the papers, as did Dorothy and Jerry. I was free to go. I heaved a sigh of relief... and the marshals walked over to Jerry, put handcuffs on him, and led him away. I knew what he would be going through; I knew it was endurable. I cried anyhow.

Later, I was walking down the sidewalk in front of the courthouse, friends on either side of me. No handcuffs, no bars, only sunlight and the traffic in the street. It held no reality for me. How could the sky be blue, when I knew it was grey? One person offered me a bag of cheese popcorn, my favorite food. I couldn't eat it. Something was very wrong.

When we arrived at the place where I'd been living before I went off to jail, another friend and jailbird was on her way out. I met her in the street. She hugged me, took a step back, took hold of me by the arms, and said, "Welcome to the free world." I stared at her uncomprehendingly and then burst into tears. She hugged me again, saying, "It's over, it's over..."

I couldn't speak; all I could do was to pull myself away and, horrified, shake my head. It wasn't over. I wasn't free. How could she, who had been there, so completely not understand? While my brothers and

sisters were still back in that dark hole of grey metal and cement, in some indefinable but very real way, I was back there with them.

I spent only five weeks in the Cass County Jail before being released, but that experience has never left me. Even now, as I write this from the Federal Correctional Institution at Alderson, West Virginia, with more than a year of prison ahead of me, I remember what it was like to leave, and I wonder how it will be the next time.—**Ariel Glenn**

The Probationer Is
Twice Guilty

BEING ON PROBATION is similar to house arrest— something even the apostle Paul put up with for a few years.

Going on probation was an option that I considered from the beginning as a participant in the Missouri Peace Planting. I planned to cooperate with the authorities enough to warrant probation, if they were in the mood to offer it. I was prepared to serve the jail time if so sentenced. But I knew that if offered probation I would certainly accept. They did, and I did.

Being home with my children, ages three and thirteen, and being happy and exhausted at the end of a day's active parenting—as only a parent can be exhausted—lets me know that I made the right choice.

What I didn't plan for, however, was the guilt. Try having a dozen or so co-conspirators all in jail, while you're out smelling the roses.

Since I've been given all this unwarranted spectacular freedom, I figure the only responsible thing to do is enjoy it. Enjoy it for twelve, even.

How do I handle the guilt?

A friend who spent three weeks in jail for trespassing at an Air Force base tells me her visitors would express guilt because she was in jail and they weren't. So here am I, who also spent three weeks in jail before going on probation, burning with guilt because my silo buddies are doing months or years. It's all relative.

My friend's point was that people in the peace movement usually feel guilty for not doing more. There's always somebody you can point to who has paid a higher price than you.

While pondering these thoughts, I opened a letter from another friend who had just been moved to a better dormitory at the prison in Lexington. You guessed it—she was feeling guilty.

I laughed out loud.

Probation means that suddenly you find yourself agreeing to cooperate with this government which has so thoroughly demonstrated itself to be uncooperative, belligerent, and against life. But there it is, and what a contradiction it is: your mission is to be peaceful, cooperative, and loving of life, even to the very face of this beast you are called to resist!

If you think you might want to try probation but aren't sure you could really handle it, remember that it has the virtue of being reversible—you can always change your mind and go back to do your jail time. It's like a "flexible start date" for your sentence—good for up to three years.

And finally, if you decide to pay your fines as part of your probation agreement, you can try taking comfort in the scriptural admonition to "accept the confiscation of your property cheerfully—knowing that you have a better inheritance yet to come." You can also remember the one who said, "if the authorities compel you to go a mile with them, go with them two." —**Gail Beyer**

Law and Order in Lafayette County

LATE ONE SATURDAY NIGHT all hell broke loose at the Lafayette County jail in Lexington, Missouri. From the cell we could hear the sounds of voices and shuffling feet as a large number of revelers were being brought in under arrest. One man didn't seem happy about the prospect of a night in jail and was not sufficiently sober to know that resistance was not a good tactic for him to follow. As we listened, the unmistakable sounds of blows told us that someone was being beaten. We were never able to find out the full details because a few minutes later one of the cops appeared at our cell and told us to pack up. We were moved to another cell block to spend the night.

We can only guess that the man who was beaten and his companions were put in the cell we vacated. When we returned the next day the cell was empty.

A word of caution: Beware attending any town celebrations in Lafayette County, Missouri, because the consequences might not be enjoyable.

We learned another lesson in Lafayette County justice one evening when the cell door opened and a teenage prisoner was brought in by a guard. The slightly built young man seemed scared. The guard told us the youngster had been threatened with rape the night before in the general jail population.

Fortunately for him, the next day was visiting day and he was able to relate the story to his mother when she came to see him. She went to the sheriff and insisted on protection for her son. So he was brought to our cell for safekeeping. If it hadn't been for the lucky timing, the young man would surely have been a victim.

Another example:

One night our sleep was disturbed by the sound of voices in an adjoining cell. The voices were those of two young men, both teenagers from a small town near St. Louis. This was their story: With a companion, they had driven west in search of wild marijuana and found a field growing along the road near Lexington. They returned after midnight to harvest what turned out to be a trunkful of the crop. The fellow who told us about it said that he was sitting in the car while the other two were harvesting when suddenly he was confronted by a bare-chested, sleepy-eyed man holding a shotgun. It turned out that the man with the gun was a deputy sheriff of Lafayette County and that the marijuana crop was on his property.—**Joe Gump**

Beware of the Black Box

WHILE IN TRANSIT from Omaha, Nebraska, to the minimum security camp attached to the Marion Federal Penitentiary in Marion, Illinois, I was told by a surly guard to recite my prison registration number. But I hadn't yet learned the number, having just been turned over to the federal marshals after a week in a county jail.

When I said "I don't know what my number is," the lieutenant got visibly angry, thinking I was a wise guy trying to make life hard for him. He grabbed my identification card from one of the marshals and read "Destination: Marion." Since Marion is the toughest of the maximum security prisons in the United States the lieutenant evidently jumped to the conclusion that

I was a hard case, not to be treated lightly. For all he knew, I was headed for the hole for life without parole.

So to teach me a lesson he reached for a "black box"—a hard plastic case about the size of a camera, with steel fittings. The box fits over the handcuffs, between the wrists, and when closed immobilizes the prisoner's hands. Padlocked to my handcuffs, which were locked to a waist chain, the box forced my arms into a fixed position near my waist, as if I were taking a photo of my thighs. It was a trick to use the urinal or eat the bag lunch they served on the prison bus.

The black box is used especially for escape artists to prevent picking of the handcuff locks. So from then on the other cons on the bus called me "Houdini," a reference to my childhood idol Harry Houdini, master magician and debunker of frauds.

A word to the wise: Resisters should avoid giving the wrong impression to a prison guard because the black box is an extremely uncomfortable device which makes any kind of relaxation either short-lived or impossible.—**John LaForge**

Mother's Day

THE CHILDREN start arriving at 8 or so in the morning at Alderson Federal Correctional Institution. This is the only day in the year they can spend alone with their mothers on the prison grounds.

Administrators, employees, and guards all participate, proud of their graciousness, their kindness, their sensitivity on this one day. The prison provides free ice cream, cotton candy, games, balls, balloons, baby animals to look at, face painting. It's like going to the fair.

Many of these children don't see their mothers often—once every two years is not unusual. Some of the younger ones don't even know who their mothers are. Because surrogate parents are not allowed in on Mother's Day, the child may be left to enjoy the day with a stranger.

Before the children are allowed in, each is patted down—even the infants. Diapers are removed in the search for drugs and other contraband.

There are some sad scenes: A young girl looks in bewilderment, trying to figure out which woman is her "mommy." A little boy screams for his mommy, unaware that she is the one holding his hand.

More anguish at the end of the day, once children and parents are reacquainted, when the time comes to leave. Mom is distraught and the kids wonder why it is that she gets to stay in such a nice place while they have to go.

Such cruelties are perpetrated to make prison administrators look and feel good, thinking they have done their part to preserve the family. They are sorely mistaken.

There's no reason why mothers in prison shouldn't be with their young children all the time. To allow just one day a year is a travesty.

As the women made the most of their fleeting moments of motherhood, and as the administration flaunted its compassion, the children absorbed another dose of psychological punishment in their battered lives. And a wonderful day was had by all.—**Bonnie Urfer**

When Suffering Hits
Rock Bottom

I WAS WALKING back to the tool warehouse, broom and rake over my shoulder, tired and sweaty from a day's work in the sun. It was Friday—almost quitting time. One week completed at Yankton Federal Prison Camp. From behind, I heard the loud forceful voice of a street fighter, "Hey man, wait up." It was "Bull"—a fellow worker on the "grounds crew"—the lowest job on the hierarchical ladder of inmate jobs. We spend most of our day "keeping busy" (as several guards openly admit) by doing almost entirely meaningless tasks—sweeping sidewalks that are barely dusty or raking the soil for no useful reason.

As Bull approached I wondered what was on his mind; his usual topics deal with all the women he's had (that's putting it politely) or the boxing matches he's won.

In a softer tone of voice than I've heard him speak, Bull asked, "Do you believe in prayer?" Surprised, hesitant, I responded, "Yeah, I sure do." He continued, "I'm convinced that prayer is the only way to beat drugs. I've been prayin' real hard lately... prayin' that I'll stay the fuck off cocaine when I get out of here... I've been calling and writing letters to my wife to get her to stop taking cocaine and heroin. She thinks I'm crazy, man. My seven-year-old daughter wrote me... I know she's hurtin' bad. She wants Ma off drugs... I've been prayin' real hard..."

I listened on, nodding in affirmation, not knowing exactly what to say. It's a powerful thing to be trusted with such tender words in this setting. Until that conversation, I had begun to feel anonymous and insignificant in prison. The arbitrary rules, the lack of privacy, the meaningless work are all designed to undermine an inmate's sense of purpose, dignity, and self-esteem. Dialogues about my being sentenced for sitting on a missile silo ended short with many inmates. Most were sympathetic in a general way but at the same time profoundly cynical about any possibility to effect change. I was fighting self-doubt—trying to convince myself that being here made a difference.

Ironically, Bull brought me strength with his pain and with his trust. It mattered to him that I was here. I didn't have to say much or have any answers; just listen. And with the listening came God's grace—a sense of redemptive intimacy with people whose suffering has hit rock bottom. Bull and I put the brooms and rakes away and headed back to the dormitory for 4 o'clock count.—**Mike Bremer**

To Work or Not to Work

SARAH BEARD, my camp counselor, frowned at the report she held in her hand and then looked at me in puzzlement and exasperation. "Tell me, Mr. Day, is this some kind of antinuclear protest?"

I shook my head. She and two other officers in the room listened carefully as I explained what had prompted me to write the letter to the camp superintendent. Their expressions told me that this case was a pain in the neck.

They put some questions, exchanged glances, then asked me to wait outside in the corridor. Minutes later, Ms. Beard stuck her head out the door and told me I could leave. I would hear from them later.

At the Yankton Federal Prison Camp, as elsewhere in the U.S. prison system, refusal to work is considered a serious offense. Taking that step was the most difficult decision of my short prison career.

It led to arrest and confinement in the local jail, expulsion from one of the most comfortable penal facilities in the country, and ultimate banishment to a world of handcuffs, ankle chains, and strip searches. The decision also brought liberation.

To work or not to work? That was a question I had begun pondering even before my sentencing to a six-month term for trespassing at a nuclear missile launch site in Missouri. Committing the trespass for me had been a form of withdrawing my consent to deployment of nuclear weapons. By the same logic, should I not also withhold cooperation from the penal system that punishes noncompliance with nuclear weapons deployment? Why play ball with the U.S. Bureau of Prisons after refusing to do so with the U.S. Air Force?

Long before going to prison I had watched others wrestle with such questions.

Richard Miller, sentenced to four years for digging up railroad tracks in the path of the "nuclear train" in Texas, had spent much of that time in the hole for refusing to work and had written eloquently about his experience in letters to his home community in Des Moines.

Joe Gump had gone to the hole at Oxford Prison Camp for refusing a work assignment. His wife Jean was in the hole in the prison at Alderson for refusing to give a urine sample in view of a guard.

I read about those and similar acts of prison resistance. After going to jail in March of 1989, knowing I would soon be facing job placement at a federal institution, I inquired about the potential consequences of refusing to work. Other inmates told me it

would mean the loss of what few freedoms and comforts could be found in prison. Most of them advised
against it.

"Just because you're working doesn't mean you
have to work your ass off," they told me. Besides, work
makes the time go faster.

It wasn't until I reached Yankton prison camp, well
into my second month of confinement, that I made up
my mind. What made noncooperation a necessity for
me was the dishonesty and injustice I found there.

Yankton was a prison masquerading as a camp. I
found no guard houses, fences, or razor wire; no bars
in the windows or locks on the dormitory doors, no
slipper-clad inmates in orange coveralls. Instead, the
constraints were in our minds. In exchange for the
freedoms and comforts of a college campus we had
agreed to be our own keepers. But we were prisoners
nonetheless. That was the dishonesty.

And at Yankton we were part of an inmate elite—
an educated, white, middle-class elite reflecting the
privileged strata of the outside world. Gone behind
penitentiary walls were the semi-literate slobs, the
ghetto drug hustlers, the desperados with whom I had
shared jail space only recently. Yankton presented a
mirror image of the inequities of the larger society,
dependent on the brute deterrence of nuclear weapons. That was the injustice I found there.

I wanted the system that had put me in prison to
deal openly and honestly with that fact, not muffle it
in camps and counselors and campuses, in fancy
recreation programs and neatly pressed khaki uniforms that made us look and feel like ROTC cadets. I
wanted to make this vast bureaucracy feed a cultivated peacenik the same shit it dishes out to spics and
niggers.

But I didn't want to sound crazy or masochistic. I wanted to be understood not only by the penal authorities but also by my fellow inmates and the outside world. So, following the advice of friends at the camp, I took my stand on a narrow issue.

In my letter to the camp superintendent, Stephen F. Pontesso, informing him of my decision to do no more institutional work, I stressed my philosophical objection to the mission of the camp, which is to prepare more bed space for the federal government's rapidly rising prison population. I also acknowledged that, with barely four months of prison time left, my decision was a pragmatic one that would not necessarily fit the circumstances of other inmates facing much longer sentences and needing to earn income from prison labor.

I wanted the inmates to understand. I wanted to test the water, to be a guinea pig, for other short-termers struggling with the question of resistance within the system. And I wanted the prison administration to take notice.

Did the message get through? I got my answer when a counselor drew me aside moments before a guard escorted me off the Yankton campus for the last time.

"Look here, Day," he said. "You keep this to yourself and you'll be o.k. But if you start stirring it around you're going to be in big trouble." —**Sam Day**

Fifteen Days in the Hole

AS AN ORDERLY assigned to clean the visiting room at the Oxford (Wisconsin) Federal Correctional Institution, the rules require that I submit to a daily strip search before and after work. That means I must take my clothes off and allow a guard to examine my orifices and hairy parts. It is a dehumanizing, unnecessary, and futile ritual. And so I decided to protest.

For the first few days on the job I got away with refusing the strip search. Most guards find the practice as distasteful as I do. But discipline at the camp was being tightened, and there came a day when one young guard felt he had to obey the rules and ordered me to remove all my clothing.

When I reached my shorts, I refused to go any further. The guard called up to the lieutenant's office and was told to handcuff me and escort me to the Detention Center.

Once there I was again ordered to strip. And once again I left my shorts on and told the officers I would go no further. I told them I was doing this for their sake as well as mine. They knew me well enough to be sure I wouldn't bring in contraband.

The officers were unmoved. Two of them took hold of my hands and pinned them against the wall while another officer pulled down my shorts and bent me over. They examined my private parts and spread the cheeks of my rump. When the search was over I was issued a single-piece tan jumpsuit, handcuffed, and led to Cell A-12 in the "Segregation" area.

For one week I was alone in the hole. They told me not to talk to other prisoners, which would have been difficult anyway since few passed by within earshot. I learned later that the man in the next cell had stabbed a fellow inmate seventeen times in the heart.

For reading and writing I had only my pocket New Testament, a pencil, some paper, and a few envelopes the first few days. I had to wait till the weekend to get stamps from the prison chaplain. Once a day I was led, handcuffed, to a walled-in courtyard for an hour of sunlight, fresh air, and the songs of birds. I walked, I jogged, I prayed. It was my favorite time of day.

The only other times I was permitted out of the hole were for occasional showers and for hearings before my counselor, my case manager, and the prison lieutenant. They warned me of the likelihood of being transferred to a higher security prison. I gave them a long written statement pleading my case.

At my disciplinary hearing the assembled staff officers, including the chaplain, who acted as my representative, told me that my refusal to submit to the strip search proved nothing and would lead only to the practice being more emphatically enforced.

Noting that I am a Franciscan father, the hearing officer told me that, here in prison, "you are not a priest." "Mr. Cowan," I replied, "here in prison I feel more like a priest than ever before." In the end, my punishment was light: an additional seven days in disciplinary segregation, six months probation, and an assurance that any further infractions of any kind would get me shipped to a stricter prison. I would have to agree to submit to the strip search on my way out of detention. It was a difficult decision, but after prayer and fasting I decided to comply. By taking a stand I had at least raised the issue of dehumanization in the prison system.

And by bowing to authority, thus avoiding transfer to a higher security prison, I had saved my parents further anxiety.

A week later, just before I was to leave the hole, Mr. Cowan came to visit me.

"I hope you're not planning to resist the strip search on your way out of here," he said.

"No, I'm not. I promised you during the hearing that I would submit to it."

"Good! The warden chewed me out for not transferring you. I had to explain it."

"Why?"

"Do you know that the two worst things an inmate can do is assault an officer or refuse a direct order?"

"How's that? There's a big difference between the two. One is a violent action and the other, ordinarily, is not."

"From an administrative point of view they are the same thing."—**Jerry Zawada**

Thanks, I Needed That

THE PRISON FARM is looked upon as the worst place to work at Terre Haute Camp. The long hours, hard work in the hot sun, and the eccentric farm manager motivate people to find other jobs lest they be assigned to the farm.

The farm manager, let's call him Mr. Jones, is a crusty, old Indiana farmer who has worked for the Bureau of Prisons (BOP) for twenty years. He is sixty-two years old, has been doing things the same way for a long time, and sees no reason to change. He is a farmer/guard from the "old school." He moves about in his gray uniform and blue BOP baseball cap with a slow, deliberate stride, running the farm as an absolute dictator.

The interaction between Mr. Jones and the prisoners is cause of much conversation when he is not around. His philosophy can be summed up in two phrases: (1) "If you act like men I'll treat you like men, if you act like inmates I'll treat you like inmates," and (2) "I never believe an inmate."

He expects us to work when there is work to do, but doesn't press us when there isn't. Sometimes he will get angry when things aren't done right, but almost never will he so much as say "good job" when they are done right.

"Shot," a forty-five-year-old inmate from Michigan, walks with a slow, painful-looking swagger, each foot seeming to sink into the ground as it lands, with his arms slowly swinging back and forth like twin pendulums.

He is a cheerful fellow with a ready smile and frequent chatter, entertaining us as we move up and down the rows of vegetables with our hoes. He loves to chatter about women, cars, and such things. We like him because he is a decent and funny dude who helps us pass the time.

One afternoon, after a long, hard day in which six or seven students from the prison camp's Diesel Mechanics School had helped us because there was no class that day, we were lining up to be counted by Mr. Jones before being allowed to leave. The mechanics students had not especially enjoyed the work but had chipped in just the same. After counting us in his careful, deliberate manner, the farm manager looked up from beneath the bill of his cap and said, "I'd like to thank all of you mechanics for helping us out, you are always welcome to come back." We chuckled over his wry humor.

As we started to walk away, Shot yelled out in mock indignation, "What are you going to do for us [the regular crew]? We worked hard all week."

"Come on back here," Mr. Jones responded.

Shot hesitated, then gingerly approached the boss. The farm manager grabbed him by the shoulders, wrapped an arm around his neck, pulled him closer, bent down, and planted a big, wet kiss on his cheek.

As Shot reeled back, wiping his face, we burst into laughter, realizing we had just witnessed that rarest of spectacles—a prison guard kissing a prisoner in appreciation of a good day's work. —**Sam Guardino**

Mother And Daughter

I STOOD IN A HALLWAY of Lexington Federal Correctional Institution with Barbara, a fellow inmate, awaiting the arrival of her sixty-two-year-old mother, sentenced to fifteen months in the same institution.

"I'm so afraid that this will bring back memories for her," Barbara confided.

"Has your mother been in prison before?" I asked.

Barbara nodded. "During World War II." Krystyna had survived three years in a Nazi concentration camp.

Now, suffering from severe rheumatoid arthritis, Krystyna can stand only for about five minutes at a time; she wheezes terribly with emphysema. She also has a hardy spirit.

Biting our nails and lips, waiting for Krystyna to be escorted out of the admissions room, Barbara and I wondered why they would keep an elderly woman in there so long.

Was there another way out? Where were they going to take her? Barbara prayed that her mother would be sent directly to the prison hospital, where she could receive the medication which surely had been taken from her.

We learned from a hall officer that she'd been assigned to a different unit, but at least it was the unit where Karen, the inmate doctor, lives. I ran to fetch Karen. When I returned I saw Barbara clutching her mother, sobbing. Krystyna could barely breathe. Her lips were blue and her face was a ghastly purple. Each step was a struggle. She had just been pulled and carried up two flights of stairs.

Initially, the officer escorting Krystyna had told Barbara, "Your mother will have to walk on her own. You know you're not allowed to touch her." But soon the officer began to realize how serious the situation was. She allowed me to take Krystyna's bag from Barbara, freeing the daughter to support her mother. Barbara and I were allowed to go "off limits" to accompany Krystyna to her assigned unit.

Once the medical staff evaluated Krystyna's condition we were able to breathe more easily. Especially after the prison authorities, in a rare display of common sense and compassion, decided that Barbara would be allowed to share a room with her mother.
—**Kathy Kelly**

Coming Out

NATURALLY, I was under the assumption that going to jail or prison was the hardest part of doing resistance. But after spending many days inside I discovered that going in was not nearly as difficult as coming out.

The first heartache is leaving friends behind in prison. We become attached to those around us—especially when we spend twenty-four hours a day with them, breathing, playing, sharing, laughing, and crying. It's a hard feeling to leave them behind in torture and pain.

In jail or prison you quickly learn how little you need for survival. Suddenly all the material fluff in life has disappeared. Every small thing—a bar of soap, a toothbrush, a comb—becomes a treasure. Necessities for health and hygiene become your most valuable possessions.

The contrast between what we need and what we think we need, so apparent in jail, teaches us that through our own greed and thoughtlessness we imprison ourselves in the outside world. We enslave ourselves to jobs we hate but can't quit, simply in order to pay for the comforts we're told we should have. Ours is a culture consisting of millions of individual prisons.

The sadness I feel in coming out of jail or prison is a second sentence lasting almost as long as the first.

There's a double pain in leaving friends behind in prison and seeing anew the self-constructed prisons on the outside. We are taught to believe that going home is a joyous occasion. The joy is accompanied by a million tears.—**Bonnie Urfer**

20

Rules For Survival

Remember: you are not alone. When times get tough, as they inevitably will, remind yourself that you are a "prisoner of conscience" in the tradition of Mohandas Gandhi and Martin Luther King, Jr. Remember that you share an important mission with other prisoners of conscience elsewhere in this country and the world. Know that your example of self-sacrifice is as likely to reach the hearts of others—to awaken interest and to strengthen commitments—as anything you have done before. Give yourself a big pat on the back as you stare out your window at "the free world." Just by being where you are you make a lasting contribution to peace and justice.

Keep your focus. Do all you can to remember who *you* are and why *you* are in jail. There will be dark, exhausting times when you are trying so hard to survive that you forget your purpose. Take a minute and refocus yourself when that happens. You may want to read an article or chapter on a social justice topic. Or reread an old letter from a friend and comrade. Or pray. Or simply walk or lie down and reflect. Or write a letter or write in your journal. Or take a nap. There are many ways to refocus; don't despair, just be positive and keep trying.

Write letters. Your status as a "prisoner on purpose" will make you an object of interest to many— your family and friends, of course, and also others who hear of your case: your doctor, a former teacher, strangers who may read about you in the newspaper. They may be worried, angry, or puzzled, but already they have made a psychological connection with the issues that prompted you to act. You should draw upon that opening. Try to deepen their understanding. Write letters. Write often. Your letters are seeds for the cause.

Don't be shy about accepting gifts. Most of our lives are spent being taught not to ask for things— it's a sign of social incompetence or begging. But those on the outside want to help and need to help. We should let them do so, especially if we have needs. Just as we give, we must learn to receive.

Dear Diary: Keep a journal or some comparable record of your thoughts. Try writing in your journal every day, even a little bit if it is late at night and you are struggling to stay awake. On some days you may write many pages.

Stay in touch. The federal prison system forbids communication with inmates at other penal institutions. Nevertheless, it is still possible for you to keep in touch with friends behind bars. This is done by writing to a friend outside, who repackages the letter. Remember that all incoming mail is examined for contraband and (except for legal mail) sometimes very thoroughly read by the authorities. So be circumspect.

Who needs possessions? They say Mohandas Gandhi got along well in life with just three belongings—his loincloth, his sandals, and his spectacles. No wonder he took so easily to jail! The same attitude will help you adjust to prison and jail in the United States. You'll always have clothes on your back (jail clothes) but sometimes not much else. When you surrender to the authorities say good-bye to your watch, your purse or wallet, your pen, your belt, your jewelry. Better memorize those important addresses and telephone numbers because your papers will be taken from you when you move. Most things that are essential to you in everyday life fall into the dreaded category of "contraband" in jail and prison. When you reach your final destination in the penal system the rules will lighten up a little; and it's easy to adjust if you simply remember that most people in the world still live with less.

Recycle everything. You just came across a small piece of tin foil? Don't throw it away—it has a thousand uses inside the pen. That pair of jeans you ripped out will make a great handbag for you or your roommate(s). In fact, just about anything you might want to toss out is probably useful to someone, somewhere.

Be proud but humble. As a "prisoner on purpose" you'll be an object of curiosity (even amusement) to your fellow inmates. Some will find it difficult to understand why you deliberately exposed yourself to arrest and imprisonment. But many will sympathize with your action and respect you for it, provided you show understanding for them. Remember that many of your new neighbors, serving terms much longer than yours, are victims of racism and oppression who never had the opportunity to be peacemakers.

Get to know the inmates. One of the best things about incarceration is the opportunity it offers to meet people from other walks of life and to better understand the systemic injustice that fills our jails and prisons with its victims. Take time to listen to your fellow prisoners. Their stories will help you connect the peace and justice issues. And their company will make your jail/prison time more fruitful and enjoyable. Card games are an excellent way to break the ice. Among the most popular inmate games are Hearts, Gin Rummy, and Spades (a derivative of Bridge).

Don't pry. Be careful about prying into other prisoners' affairs, such as the reason they are in jail, and their family problems. Most of your fellow prisoners will readily talk about their legal cases—in fact, it is the leading topic of conversation (other than sex). But it's a good rule to wait for someone to offer that information. Or raise the subject yourself by saying, "Do you mind if I ask you what you are in here for?" Many prisoners have bad family situations. There is a lot of loneliness for people away from their spouses and children. You will be moved by the sight of inmates in the visiting room with children whom they can see only once in a great while. Be sensitive—interested in other people's lives and always willing to listen. But don't be nosy.

Be yourself. Don't try too hard to be like your fellow prisoners in order to be closer to them. They will respect you for being yourself, although at times you will feel a little left out if you are the only one in the cell not reading *Playboy*.

Stay healthy. Eat as well as possible wherever you are. That is difficult in many jails and prisons, but do your best to keep up your strength. Make sure that you are getting at least a minimum amount of nutrition, even when the food doesn't taste good.

How to beat the smoke. Try breathing through a wet washcloth if the cigarette smoke becomes overwhelming. Since smoke rises, the lower portions of the room will likely be the clearest. Try sitting on the floor with your washcloth and a good book.

Try kicking those habits. Whatever else may be said about it, incarceration does offer you a change in lifestyle. If you happen to be a smoker, this could be your golden chance—free of customary social tensions—to kick that habit. A prisoner's dependence on tobacco puts leverage in the hands of the guards. Kicking the tobacco (and junk food) habit can also free up your limited commissary budget for more important items—such as stamps, envelopes, and writing paper with which to "kick the Bomb."

Stay on the ball. Determine to devote free time to keeping mentally and physically fit. Do yoga, physical fitness, aerobic exercise, diet discipline; take education courses. Prison is a good place to learn a second language (especially Spanish) and to brush up on arts and crafts, carpentry, welding, auto mechanics, or public speaking.

Stretch those muscles. You may find yourself stuck in a county jail or in holdover with nothing to do for long periods of time. If so, try hanging from the bars by your hands every now and then. This stretches muscles that have gotten stiff from all-day all-week sitting around. Very relaxing.

It helps to laugh. Don't take prison life too seriously—resist by laughing at it a lot.

It helps to sing. Take one day at a time and sing a song each day.

Make your own sound. Bring your Walkperson with you. It is effective for blocking out noises. If you bring the right music, you just might wind up dancing.

The chapel beckons. A lot of the preaching in prisons tends to be Christian fundamentalist, but there are exceptions. And chapel can be a place to get away from the tension. Even when you disagree with what the chaplain has to say, you still may find him to be a prisoner's friend rather than a yes-man for the administration.

Prison etiquette. Good manners and common sense will keep you clear of tight spots. Intense overcrowding makes inmates very sensitive about personal space. Say excuse me when you bump or accidentally touch another inmate. If you have a top bunk, *do not* step on the bottom bunk when climbing up or down. Always knock before entering another person's room. Even if not a word is spoken at the dinner table, always say excuse me when you get up to leave. Never go into another person's room if that person is not present. Be careful about borrowing from others and promptly repay *all* debts. In a group of people, never unilaterally change the television channel. Keep your living area neat and orderly. Be generous, but don't let people take undue advantage of your kindness. In an argument, graciously conceding defeat avoids dangerous escalations over petty matters.

Space is precious. Don't mess with anyone's stuff—even innocently. The little space that prisoners are able to get for themselves is precious.

Be a team player. Remember that you are a prisoner just like everyone else with whom you are incarcerated. You are all in it together, no matter what brought you to jail. No one is any better or worse; you are all prisoners.

Carry your own load. Whatever your decision may be about accepting institutional work assignments, be sure to carry your own load with your fellow inmates. Keep yourself and your personal space clean and neat and do at least your fair share of the daily housecleaning. This will help relations with your neighbors and eliminate some unnecessary hassles from the guards.

Expect travel hassles. Some of the worst annoyances and indignities of penal life are associated with travel. These include being chained by the wrists, waist, and ankles; frequent strip searches and changes of clothing; not knowing where you're going until you get there, and being cut off from friends and relatives while in transit. In county jails and in transient "holdover" cells you are usually "locked down" and allowed a minimum of privileges and personal possessions. Generally, things get better when you reach your final destination in the penal system.

Read the book. As a new prisoner you will be given a thick booklet of rules and regulations. It is wise to know the rules even though many are not enforced. Better to know in advance what the consequences of resistance will be than to get slapped with extra duty or worse out of ignorance.

Look before you leap. Learn about the "justice system" before you challenge it. Pick your challenges carefully and wisely. You can't challenge it every day, nor can you challenge everything that happens.

Watch those guards. Try to be understanding and patient with the staff, recognizing that they are human beings in difficult, almost impossible jobs. At the same time, keep a sharp eye on the guards and staff because they have the power to hurt you. Never trust them with sensitive information—remember that their first allegiance is always to the Bureau of Prisons. Being a prison guard brings out the worst in many, but some guards and other staff treat prisoners with respect and restraint.

Don't buddy up to a guard. Be careful in relating to guards. Even simple politeness can be construed by other inmates as "snitch" activity. Being perceived as either a snitch or a friend of the hacks can definitely be hazardous to your health in prison.

Be on guard. Remember that jails are filled with snitches who are looking for a way out, meaning they are eager to turn on a fellow inmate in return for special privileges or, more importantly, a sentence reduction. Remember, too, that frequently inmates will lie about their crimes and personal history.

Beware of the telephone. In jail and prison the telephone is an instrument of pain as well as pleasure. In addition to letters and occasional visits, it is the means of maintaining contact with friends and loved ones. But availability of telephones varies a lot from one institution to another. Even in the best of places you can sometimes wait hours to make a call. In other places, especially county jails, you can wait a week or longer for the privilege of competing with a dozen others for precious telephone time. Calls, incidentally, are always collect. The telephone is a frequent source of friction in jail and prison. But don't take your frustration out on the poor soul who may have beaten you out of a few minutes on the phone. Complain to the people in charge.

Stay in control; follow your own agenda. Jails and prisons try to break your independent spirit, undermine your self-respect, teach you who is boss. There will be dozens of rules, some of them nonsensical and erratically enforced. But that doesn't mean you must surrender your conscience, your mind, your energy, your commitment to the principles that put you behind bars. Whatever your jail/prison duties, you will have time left over for your own peace-and-justice work. Use it. Take time out for fun, to be sure, but set your own agenda for doing what you want done. Put jail and prison to work for you.

21

Peace Planters '88

Duane Bean, 31, Chicago, Illinois. In 1979, while a communications major at Northwestern University, he co-founded a group called Students for the Re-establishment of American Pride whose sole purpose was the staging of a media event entitled the "I Love America Rally." Served as a national advance man for Ronald Reagan's 1980 presidential campaign. Worked for two years in advertising. Enlisted in the Illinois National Guard as a combat medic. At the University of Illinois-Chicago, he worked as a political science teaching assistant and lay campus minister. He was also active in the environmental movement, volunteered in a shelter for the homeless and in 1987 signed the Pledge of Resistance. His involvement with the Chicago Pledge led to several arrests for protests against U.S. intervention in Central America. A week before the Missouri Peace Planting he and twenty-two others were arrested for blockading the entrance to Williams International, Inc., a manufacturer of engines for the cruise missile located outside Detroit, and received a thirty day suspended jail sentence. On August 15, 1988, he and Franciscan priest Jerry Zawada entered missile launch site G11 in Missouri, poured blood, and celebrated a Eucharistic liturgy.

Arrested for five missile silo entries in Missouri, he was tried, convicted, and received a one year sentence, which he served at the Chicago Metropolitan Correctional Center.

"People always ask what they can do to help me in prison. Increasingly I am convinced that the most subversive thing we can do is to begin asking questions. We are all prisoners of oppressive social, economic, and personal relationships. But each time we simplify our lifestyles, engage in ecologically responsible consumption, educate ourselves about local/global human rights issues, we are acting out of a sense of deep personal responsibility. Each compassionate action expands our capacity to love, removes our fear, and creates a great, irresistible ripple that ruptures the facade of indifference, ignorance, and complacency."

Gail Beyer, 37, Madison, Wisconsin, is a computer programmer for the State of Wisconsin and mother of two daughters. She has been involved in antinuclear resistance since 1980. For six years she has been a regular vigiler with Vigil for Peace, a weekly antinuclear presence at the U.S. Internal Revenue Service office in Madison.

Gail was arrested with Bonnie Urfer at missile launch site K6 on August 15, 1988. On August 28, 1988—the twenty-fifth anniversary of the "I Have a Dream" march in Washington, D.C.—she and Bonnie joined Kathy Kelly and Duane Bean at silo C4. For her crime U.S. Magistrate Calvin Hamilton offered her three years probation, 200 hours community service, twenty days in jail, and a fine. She accepted.

Gail copes with her grief about the world's conditions by actively hoping and working for a nuclear-free world. Her faith in a loving God provides her with courage to continue. As part of her hope for the world, Gail works at getting the nukes out of her own life. Her home is wood-heated; the refrigerator stays unplugged most of the time; she does not drive. She has recently acquired a bicycle with a cart in the back, to haul the three-year-old.

Michael J. Bremer, 30, Chicago, Illinois, is a self-employed carpenter and Central America peace activist. For two years he traveled extensively in Central America. In 1986 he worked as a long-term volunteer with Witness for Peace in Nicaragua—traveling in areas of conflict and documenting the effects of the U.S.-contra war upon civilians. On August 17, 1988, the third day of Peace Planting '88, he and eight fellow resisters entered missile launch site N2, near Lexington, Missouri. They sang and prayed on the silo lid until local authorities arrested them.

At his sentencing, Bremer proposed to Judge John T. Maughmer a sentence of community service in Nicaragua in order to "serve as a form of compensation that the U.S. government owes to that country." Challenging the court to recognize the Nuremberg principles, he stated, "In a world teeming with weapons of mass destruction in the first world and hungry children in the third world, an understanding and respect for international law on the part of our nation's citizens is essential to our survival... Perhaps we as citizens need to be the first to put the question before you: What responsibility do judges have in regard to nuclear weapons policies? How long can our courts carry on as if international law did not exist?" Judge Maughmer refused to consider the proposal and did not respond to the questions. Refusing probation, Bremer was sentenced to six months at Yankton Federal Prison Camp, Yankton, South Dakota.

Samuel H. Day, Jr., 61, Madison, Wisconsin, is co-director of Nukewatch, former editor of *The Bulletin of the Atomic Scientists* and managing editor of *The Progressive*; editor of *Nuclear Heartland*, a book about

the 1,000 missiles of the U.S. Strategic Air Command. He is married, with three sons and two grandchildren. Sam entered missile launch site K8 near Rich Hill, Missouri, on August 15, 1988, dressed in a clown costume. Charged with trespass, tried and convicted, he was given the maximum sentence of six months in prison. On May 24 he was expelled from Yankton Federal Prison Camp for refusing to work. Transferred to other institutions, Day continued his work refusal and spent most of the remainder of his sentence in disciplinary segregation.

From his statement to Judge Joseph E. Stevens, Jr. at the time of sentencing: "I entered Site K8 to call attention to the danger posed by the missile underneath, and to register personal opposition to the governmental policy which goes by the name of nuclear deterrence but is in truth a policy of global intimidation aimed at maintaining a privileged life for some at the expense of others... This is not the first chapter in the story of nonviolent resistance... Nor will it be the last. Together, and in all humility, we hope to give the judges of the Western District of Missouri many more opportunities to reconsider their responsibilities. With your help, and with God's help, we will overcome."

Dorothy Eber, 62, Villa Park, Illinois, is the mother of four and grandmother of eleven. She is a minister of care at St. Pius parish and Elmhurst Hospital, has worked with Hope Fair Housing Center in DuPage County and tutored teen-aged youths, and is active with Disarm Now Action Group.

With other Peace Planters, Dorothy entered five missile silo launch sites in Missouri in August, 1988. Each time she went past the gates of a silo, she carried a cross. She is motivated by her faith in God and the conviction that she is called to say No to violence and to nuclear weapons. Arrested, tried, and convicted, she was sentenced to twenty-six months in prison, including two months for contempt of court for refusing to identify other participants. She was sent to the Lexington (Kentucky) federal prison.

Katey Feit, 26, Chicago, with Sam Guardino, climbed the fence of missile launch site K10. With the sun rising over the surrounding hay fields they planted iris bulbs, scattered bird seed and wild strawberry seeds, and prayed. Their actions were witnessed by Margaret and Thomas Montgomery. Katey was charged with trespass, tried, convicted, and given the maximum sentence of six months in prison. She served her sentence at the Chicago Metropolitan Correctional Center.

Laura Ariel Glenn, 27, is a community member at Casa Maria Catholic Worker House in Milwaukee, Wisconsin, where women and families in need of shelter and food are welcomed.

She is a veteran of the U.S. Army and was honorably discharged in 1982 after a three-year hitch. Ariel has been involved in peace and justice issues since the early 1980s and has lived at Casa Maria for two years.

In August, 1988, she was arrested and charged with three trespasses for entering nuclear missile launch sites in Missouri. She was sentenced to nineteen months in prison and sent to the Federal Correctional Institution in Alderson, West Virginia. In prison she provided legal help to other inmates.

Sam Guardino, 29, lives and works in Chicago's Uptown neighborhood. Employed by the Lakefront SRO Corporation, a not-for-profit housing organization which provides decent, affordable housing for low income single people, he is also involved with the

St. Francis Catholic Worker House. Sam entered missile launch site K10 in Bates County, Missouri, with Katey Feit, on August 15, 1988. They planted strawberries and flowers, spread bird seed, prayed, read poetry, walked around the inside of the fence, and sat on the silo lid in order to reclaim that piece of land for the peaceful purpose for which it was intended. Charged with trespass, tried, and convicted, he was given the maximum sentence of six months by Federal Judge Joseph E. Stevens, Jr. He spent his time at the Terre Haute, Indiana Federal Prison Camp, where he planted vegetables on the prison farm.

Sam told Judge Stevens at the conclusion of his trial: "Each time someone has been thrown in jail for missile silo actions, more people have followed to trespass on the silos. I believe that will continue to happen."

Kathy Kelly, 36, Chicago, Illinois, has been a high school teacher for twelve years, and is active with the Chicago Catholic Worker and with efforts to resist U.S. intervention in Central America. She is married to Karl Meyer. Kathy entered five nuclear missile launch sites between August 15 and August 28, 1988, in the Missouri missile fields. She planted corn and attempted to tie the lids of some sites with ribbon, symbolizing desire to prevent use of the weapons. Charged with five counts of trespass, tried, and convicted, she was given one year in prison which she served in the maximum security facility for women, Lexington FCI, in Kentucky.

From her opening remarks to Judge Calvin Hamilton at the time of sentencing:

"Oliver Wendell Holmes said that freedom of speech does not permit us to shout 'Fire' in a crowded theater, when there is no fire. We have not done so.

"We have shouted 'Murder' at fifteen of the very sites where the Auschwitz of our generation begins.

"Please don't forget that these missiles are all targeted for launching... If just one of the thousand now in place were launched, the accident at Chernobyl and the Armenian earthquake would appear as minor mishaps in comparison. In the grimmest of times, these missiles have been described as 'Auschwitz to go.'

"Shall we be compliant in our generation as the Germans were in theirs?"

Betty Lewis, 61, lives in Chicago with her husband and four of her seven children. In June, 1983, after twenty frustrating years of working to end the arms race by legislative change, she decided to "put the body on the line" and became part of the nonviolent direct action movement. In 1985, the harshness of sentences imposed on missile silo activists "so no one would come back to the silos in Missouri" inspired her to follow their example.

On August 15, 1988, she climbed the fence at missile launch site L9; placed a white rose on the silo lid for protesters who were executed in Nazi Germany (the White Rose Collective) and a red rose for the Plowshares activists who had occupied and damaged missile launch sites; planted corn for the hungry, a tree for housing the homeless, and a geranium for the beauty of life; and hung a banner which read: "Because... we cannot say... we did not know." Two days later, along with eight others, she entered launch site N2 in a continuing effort to make people aware of the issues.

She pleaded no contest and was sentenced to six months in prison.

Dan McGuire, 30, Chicago, Illinois, is a member of the Oblate Connections lay volunteer community, and was married in April, 1989. He was born into a Nebraska farm family of fifteen children. Dan entered a Missouri missile silo compound on August 16, 1988, placing there a flower and a picture of his nieces and nephews. He decided not to comply with the court summons and is awaiting further action by the federal government.

"As a continuation of past acts of resistance, as a commitment to a safer world, and as a member of a dominant and ruthless race and society, I decided to do my small part by putting myself on the line and saying No to a carefree way of life and a careless culture. This is not the first time I have chosen not to comply. I do not feel guilty of a crime. And I wanted to continue the action in a way which would redirect my energy from that of going along with the system to continued community building and an interconnected awareness with oppressed people around the world."

Michael A. Stanek, 22, is a member of Oblate Connections community in Chicago, dedicated to helping homeless and poor people. He is also a member of the Industrial Workers of the World Union, "forming the structure of the new society within the shell of the old." He became an activist in high school in Pocatello, Idaho.

He occupied missile launch site K11 on August 15, 1988, with Tim Cordon as witness. Denied a jury trial, he was tried by a judge and convicted on January 17, 1989, his birthday. He was sentenced to six months in prison and sent to the Terre Haute (Indiana) Federal Prison Camp.

Bonnie Urfer, 37, Madison, Wisconsin, is a co-director of Nukewatch and co-founder of the Women's Jail Project in Madison, which supports and works with women incarcerated in the Dane County Jail. Single, from a family of three brothers and one sister, she enjoys long bicycle trips and takes her sketch pad along.

Bonnie Urfer entered three nuclear missile launch sites in Missouri in August, 1988. She was charged with three counts of trespass and two counts of depredation of government property—cutting Air Force locks. She pleaded no contest rather than participate in the violence of a trial. She was sentenced to nineteen months imprisonment, an additional six months imprisonment suspended, and three years of probation. She was sent to the federal prison in Lexington, Kentucky, and later transferred to the prison in Alderson, West Virginia.

Katie Willems, 26, Milwaukee, is a staff member at Casa Maria Catholic Worker House, a shelter for homeless women and children and a center for non-violent resistance to U.S. intervention in Central America and nuclear weapons; she also works as a word processor and is creator of a comic strip called "Wolfhounds for Peace."

Katie entered missile launch site K8 near Rich Hill, Missouri, on August 15, 1988. She played a recorder and tied balloons to missile silo fixtures. After her release and a day of rest and prayer, she returned to missile launch site N2, where she was arrested again. Katie was charged with two counts of trespass, tried, convicted. She was sentenced to six months in prison.

"I have found that I can no longer reconcile my faith in truth, nonviolence, and love with my silent complicity with the nuclear arsenal. The solution was to cease my cooperation and begin opposing these weapons directly. Now facing six months of confinement at the government's expense, I remain cheerful. Even in jail, I will be free to follow my conscience, to live in love and resist injustice as I am called to do."

Jerry (Jerome A.) Zawada, 51, Franciscan priest, Milwaukee, Wisconsin, spent the first six years of his priesthood in the Philippines; then in the inner city of Chicago and Rockford, Illinois; and in the Rio Grande Valley in southern Texas, where he became acquainted with the plight of refugees coming from Central America. Returning to the Midwest in 1984, he became involved politically with justice/peace issues in Chicago and Milwaukee while continuing parish work.

Jerry has had several trespass arrests in Chicago; at CIA headquarters at Langley, Virginia; at the nuclear weapons test site at Mercury, Nevada; at the military training site at Arlington Heights, Illinois, and at the federal building in Milwaukee. He has been arrested at demonstrations pertaining to Central America and nuclear weapons policies, apartheid in South Africa, and homeless in Milwaukee and throughout the nation.

He entered four missile launch sites in Missouri in August, 1988, and a fifth in October. Tried and convicted by a jury, he was sentenced to twenty-five months, including one month for contempt of court for refusing to say who had driven him to the silos.

After spending three months in Missouri county jails he was sent to the Oxford (Wisconsin) Federal Prison Camp. He spent fifteen days in solitary confinement for refusal to submit to daily strip searches required by his camp job.

"With our first occupation of nuclear missile silos on August 15, 1988, I felt we were on the threshold of something really exciting. We knew then that we *can* disarm the missiles with our bodies and with strong determination. I have no hesitancy in calling this effort a 'conspiracy.' As the banner placed on the silo gate during my St. Francis Day occupation (October 4, 1988) proclaimed: 'We're part of a Conspiracy of Love... With the God of the oppressed... With people of conscience... All over the world.' "

22
Glossary

ADMINISTRATIVE SEGREGATION: the "hole," but less severely restricted than disciplinary segregation.

AIN'T GOT NOTHING COMING: i.e., good time, halfway house, furlough. "Don't worry, you ain't got nothing coming." (So you can't get it taken away!)

AUTHORIZED PUBLICATION: packages containing paperback books and magazines sent to inmates must carry this label. Newspapers and hardback books are not "authorized" unless sent directly from the publisher.

BALD HEAD: someone who is naive about or easily duped by the prison system.

BEAT UP: old and ugly, e.g., "we got beat up food for dinner."

BEEFER: snitch.

BOARD (the): Parole Board.

BOOKS: inmate bank account, used for commissary purchases. "I got no money on my books."

BOP: Bureau of Prisons.

BOX: belongings sent in from the outside.

BP 8, 9, and 10: the forms used for a system of grievances which inmates may file.

BREAK: to be weak, to succumb.

BRINGING IT TO THE DOOR: completing one's full term; expirating.

BUCK: to refuse an order by a guard or staff member; to file a complaint against a guard or staff member.

BULL-DYKE: lesbian or, as a verb, lesbian activity.

BUNKIE: the person who shares a bunkbed with you. The bottom bunk is sought after and generally goes to the inmate with higher seniority.

CAMPING: serving time in a prison camp.

CAVITY SEARCH: to probe the rectum and/or vagina, looking for drugs; sometimes used to harass inmates who persist in bucking the system.

CELLIE: roommate, cellmate.

CHECK IN: to turn oneself in to protective custody within the prison (this is done by inmates who are threatened by other inmates).

CHILLIN': to lie around, relax.

CHILL OUT: to calm down or slow down; to work more slowly.

COMMISSARY: the prison store, where inmates who have money on their books may purchase toiletries, stationery, junk food, and miscellaneous other items.

CONTACT VISIT: Inmates and visitors are allowed to meet face to face, without a glass barrier, and to touch. Contact visits are standard in prison; usually they are denied in county jails, except for lawyers and ministers.

CONTROL UNIT: The most serious form of punishment for a federal prisoner is to be placed into a control unit, which is a highly restrictive setting depriving the prisoner of privileges, freedom within the institution, and contact with other prisoners. Used for extremely violent prisoners, and also sometimes for political prisoners or "troublemakers."

COP-OUT: inmate request form.

COUNT: a headcount of inmates by guards or staff; prisoners must stay in assigned places during count, or until the count is "cleared." Violations of this rule are quite serious.

CRIB: your house or apartment on the outside.

DIESEL THERAPY: a form of punishment in which the prisoner is put on the BOP transport system and shuttled from prison to jails and holding facilities all over the country.

DIME: a ten-year sentence.

DIRTY URINE: a positive test result for drugs in one's urine.

DISCIPLINARY SEGREGATION: the hole; a form of punishment usually involving solitary confinement and restricted privileges.

DOG OR ROAD DOG: a friend, companion; someone to be trusted.

DOWN ("How long have you been down?"): behind the walls; incarcerated in a closed institution.

DROP A URINE: to provide a urine specimen. Refusal to drop a urine is a serious offense.

DRY CELL: for suspected drug possessors, a cell with no sink or toilet. All waste goes into a bedpan and is inspected by guards.

EARS ("let me borrow your ears"): radio with head-phones.

EIGHT NUMBERS: refers to the eight-digit registration number given to all federal prisoners, and denotes prisoner status, e.g., "you got eight numbers, just like me."

EXPIRATE: to do one's full term without the benefit of "good time," parole, or time in halfway houses.

FCI: Federal Correctional Institution; more restrictive than a camp, but less restrictive than a penitentiary.

FIN: a five-year sentence.

GENERIC MEN: term used in women's prisons for women who appear mannish.

GETTING SHIPPED: to be punished by transfer to another, usually more restrictive, prison or jail.

GOOD TIME: time off your sentence for "good behavior."

HACK: prison guard.

HOLDOVER: a place to be held while in transit from one institution to another, or an inmate who is in transit.

HOLE: punishment; segregation, administrative or disciplinary.

HOMIE / HOME BOY: friend, partner; someone from your hometown, e.g., "Homie, doncha know me," esp. on commissary day.

HOOD: your neighborhood, where you are from.

HOUSE (my): my cell.

INCIDENT REPORT: see "SHOT"

JOINT: Prison. An FCI or a penitentiary may be referred to as "the joint," but generally a camp is not.

KITE: inmate request form in a county jail.

LEGAL MAIL: mail from lawyers, which is not to be opened and read by prison staff.

LOCKDOWN: to be locked into your cell or barracks.

LOP: connotes a weak, immature inmate; also someone who has become convinced by prison authorities of the virtues of the prison system. E.g., "Look at those fuckin' lops run for an extra scoop of ice cream."

M.R. DATE: Mandatory Release Date; full time, with no credit for good time. To "MR" is to "Bring it to the door," i.e., do your full sentence.

NICKEL: a five-year sentence.

PAPER: probation, suspended sentence. Ollie North only got paper, not jail time.

PAT-DOWN: Search of the clothed person.

POP: any male inmate over fifty.

PRESUMPTIVE DATE: the date you'll get out assuming you get all your good time.

PROTECTIVE CUSTODY: a segregated unit for snitches, who might be killed or injured if they were in general population.

R & D: Receiving and Discharge, where people are processed coming in or leaving the institution.

ROLL OVER: to inform on someone, to snitch.

RUNNING WILD: Consecutive sentences of imprisonment, as opposed to concurrent, or sentences which run simultaneously. "I got two nickels running wild," or I have two consecutive five-year sentences, for a total of ten years.

SABLE COBIE: another name for snitch, derived from the TV show "Dynasty."

SCREW: a prison guard; term originated in the days when the guards would crank the "screw jack" on the cell door manually.

SHAKEDOWN: a search of one's cell and belongings for contraband.

SHANK: homemade knife.

SHIV: sharp, pointed instrument used as a weapon.

SHORT/SHORTS: cigarette butts; e.g., "can I have your shorts?"

SHORT/SHORT-TIMER: If you don't have much time left to do, you're short, or a short-timer.

SHOT: a disciplinary incident report; "Did you get a shot for that?"

SNITCH: an inmate who has testified against another criminal defendant, or who in some other way cooperated with law enforcement authorities.

SQUARE: cigarette; peace activist inmate.

STREET: where everybody wants to go.

STRIP SEARCH: Remove your clothes, brush your hair with your hands, open your mouth, show your ears, spread fingers, raise arms to reveal armpits, lift scrotum, turn around and show the soles of both feet; bend over, spread your cheeks, squat and cough.

THROW IT DOWN: "The parole board threw it down"; you won't get parole, you'll do your full term.

WALLS: the walls of a prison. A prisoner is said to have gone behind the walls.

WAVE: rectal finger probe to search for contraband.

WHACK: to kill.

Afterword

I WAS ASKED to write about prison as a lifelong commitment. Without giving the matter much thought, I agreed, but after attempting to apply myself to the task for several days, I find that I can't. I think maybe that stems from the fact that I've now done a total of sixty-seven months of jail/prison time. If you were to ask a couple on their wedding day what marriage means to them, they might offer all kinds of explanations which, depending upon their proclivities, could be couched in romantic, philosophical, or religious terms. Ask them again five and a half years later, and I'd guess there'd be fewer words. "Marriage" is no longer external to them; it *is* their lives, and its meaning is to be found in the content of their lives which cannot be reduced to words. The wedding day images may well have had some validity, but until they are personalized through experience they are merely ideas, and once personalized, the ideas fade.

And so I think it is with the "prison witness." Reams have been written about its spiritual dimensions, and I (to my present regret) have contributed more than my share, but one's experience and perception of that and its meaning in one's daily life depend on so many complex personal factors that it cannot be translated into a formula or model of general applicability. Perhaps one reason why so many marriages fail is that so much has been written on the subject that couples figure their relationship isn't working because it doesn't feel like that for them. Has an ideal of "witness" been held up for resisters also that leaves them disillusioned when they don't experience it that way?

If anything, I'd like to demystify the whole business. Prison is just another way to live with all the elements of any other kind of living. There are the nitty-gritty aspects of physical life, some comfortable, some not. There are relationships—with people you love and those you can't stand. There are injustices, confrontations with illicit power, fun, laughter, and tragedies, and there is the inner self—mind, emotions, spirit—which is affected by and yet transcends the environment. So where is all that not so? Those are elements basic to human life, and prisoners can and do respond to them exactly as people do on the outside, and they change and grow in their response exactly as people do on the outside.

And my final reason for not being able to write on the subject is precisely that. I have changed over the years so that the purpose I now perceive for my being here, both personally and in terms of resistance, has little connection with what brought me here originally.

I think if people contemplating resistance feel the need to know something of prison life beforehand, the factual part of the foregoing book will serve them well, i.e., the descriptions of institutions in the form of a Triple A guide. The why's and how's of it are the mystery that will work itself out in unique ways for each individual. I chose it, and I am happier and stronger in my "commitment" than when I began. There is no reason to think it will be the same for others and no reason to think it won't. The bottom line is that illegal resistance (whether civil disobedience or clandestine) is likely to put you in prison, and prison, unlike modern marriage, is not something you can automatically opt out of if you decide you don't like it. The old con's adage, "Don't do the crime if you

can't do the time," is where I'd like to see the emphasis
for first-timers. The rest will come later, in its own
good time.

Helen Dery Woodson
Federal Correctional Institution
Mariana, Florida
August, 1989

Other Nukewatc

TIME BOMB (1980), A collection of articles from *The Progressive* on nuclear power and nuclear weapons, including *The H-Bomb Secret*, by Howard Morland, subject of an historic First Amendment suit.

BASIC TRAINING: A Consumer's Guide to the Military (1982), edited by Steve Meirs.

NUCLEAR HEARTLAND: A Guide to the 1,000 Missile Silos of the United States (1988), edited by Samuel H. Day, Jr., with a foreword by Philip Berrigan.

For a catalogue of Nukewatch books, maps, postcards, T-shirts, and other educational materials, write: Nukewatch, P.O. Box 2658, Madison, WI 53701. Nukewatch is a nuclear disarmament nonprofit public interest group sustained by contributions and merchandise sales.